The Modern Rite

Klaus Gamber

The Modern Rite

Collected Essays
on the Reform of the Liturgy

Translated by Henry Taylor

Saint Michael's Abbey Press
MMII

Saint Michael's Abbey Press
Saint Michael's Abbey
Farnborough
Hants. GU14 7NQ

Telephone +44 (0) 1252 546 105
Facsimile +44 (0) 1252 372 822
www.farnboroughabbey.org
prior@farnboroughabbey.org

Original edition
Ritus Modernus
Gesammelte Aufsätse zur Liturgiereform
Studia Patristica et Liturgica 4
Institutum Liturgicum Ratisbonense
© Freidrich Pustet Regensburg 1972

English translation & edition
© Scott M P Reid 2002

Translated and published by kind permission
of the Institutum Liturgicum Ratisbonense

ISBN 0 907077 37 4

A catalogue record for this book is available from the British Library.

Printed and bound in Great Britain by Biddles Ltd,
Guildford and King's Lynn.

Table of Contents

Preface

In June 1971 all the daily papers in West Germany,
for the most part in sensationalised exaggeration, carried
accounts of a "Mass Festival" in the church at Hofheim.
One of these read as follows:

In one hand they held lighted cigarettes, and in the other
the host. All round the altar were crates of beer and lem-
onade. After the consecration there was drinking, danc-
ing and flirting. Beat and Soul music got things going like
at a good party. The "Mass Festival," which lasted sixty
hours, was celebrated just recently by 700 youths and girls
from the "Union of Catholic Youth," together with the dis-
trict youth chaplain, Herbert Leuniger, in the Church of St
Boniface at Hofheim, in the Taunus, and parts of it were
broadcast on television.

How far this report corresponds to what really happened, I have no way of knowing. By and large, however,
it is probably accurate, so eyewitnesses say. I am willing
enough to accept that the priest who started this "Mass Festival" (what a dreadful name!) was motivated entirely by
good intentions, and was trying to find new ways of bringing the Mass to the young people of today. What happened
shows just what continual experimentation can lead to, that
is, to complete liturgical anarchy.

The following collection of essays by me, almost all
of which have appeared in the past two years, are intended
to draw attention to the dangers of liturgical reform from
the point of view of a historian of Liturgy, and to look
for a middle way between rigid immobility within the old
Tridentine forms, and an aimless pursuit of novelty. The
essay at the end of this little volume, which was written
while the Council was still in session, shows how I imagine
an ecumenical liturgy of the future. I have dealt with this

more fully in my book, *Liturgie übermorgen. Gedanken zur Geschichte und Zukunft des Gottesdienstes"* [Liturgy the Day after Tomorrow: Thoughts on the History and the Future of Worship] (Herder, Freiburg, 1966).

Klaus Gamber

The Difficulties
in Reforming the Liturgy[1]

Most pastors today are in agreement that a renewal of the Roman rite, which since the Council of Trent had congealed in a mass of rubricism, was long overdue. They are also agreed that the Constitution on the Sacred Liturgy issued by the Second Vatican Council to a great extent corresponds to the reasonable demands of the present day. The verdict upon the reform of the Liturgy which has been carried through in the meantime, and above all on the new liturgical books, which in recent years have been put together by a group of specialists and have been approved by Rome, is however less than unanimous.

Some reject these books as an artificial novelty. Too little account has been taken in them, they say, of tradition, nor of the insights of liturgical research. They maintain that the renewal has been taken too far. Others, again, lament that the narrow framework of rubricism has still not been overcome, and that untried and even questionable elements have thereby been set fast.

The ideas which found expression in the Council's Constitution on the Liturgy were those of the liturgical movement of the twenties and thirties; above all, the thinking of Romano Guardini and of Pius Parsch. The former was a subtle thinker who traced out the inner logic of worship, the latter a zealous pastor who wished to lead churchgoers to an appreciation of the Roman missal and of the daily offices. Neither of them, however, actually carried on original research in the history of worship. Above all, they lacked any close contact with the Liturgy of the Eastern Church, in which the early forms have been far better preserved than in the West.

In the years during which the liturgical movement was blossoming, liturgical studies were still in their

---

1. A revised version of my article, "Fehlformen und Gefahren der liturgischen Erneuerung" [Distortions and Dangers in Liturgical Renewal] in *Lebendige Seelsorge*, no. 22 (1971) pp. 67-72.

infancy. There were hardly any chairs in this subject at the universities. Liturgy was regarded above all as a matter of rubrics and ritual detail, and as such was seen as part of pastoral studies. Those few scholars who had interested themselves in the history of worship, such as G. Morin, C. Mohlberg or A. Dold, to name some among them, had for the most part no professorial chairs. Their sphere of influence was therefore limited. At any rate, those in pastoral practice were aware of hardly any of the results of their research.

Not until about ten years ago did liturgical studies eventually begin to make up for lost time. A systematic study of the sources was set in hand. Not least, more and more of the rich heritage of the Eastern liturgies was revealed to us. The significance of Christian archaeology for the history of Liturgy also became increasingly clear.

Into the midst of this hopeful beginning fell the Council's command to the specialists to reshape the forms of worship. This was without doubt asking too much of the new discipline of liturgical studies, whose research in many areas, quite understandably, could offer no definitive conclusions. What J.A. Jungmann has set forth in his *Missarum Sollemnia*[2] is simply a summary of these provisional results. This knowledge was, however, insufficient to enable a reworking of the forms of worship of any permanent value.

As far as clergy and people were concerned, things were even worse at the beginning of the process of liturgical reform. They simply were not ready for the innovations. Worship had hitherto been characterised by traditional forms and ancient customs. The participation of the faithful in the official Liturgy was normally slight. Only a few followed the Mass in their bilingual copy of "Schott."[3] There had, accordingly, been that much more luxuriant a growth

---

2. J.A. Jungmann, *Missarum Sollemnia. Eine genetische Erklärung der römischen Messe* (Herder, Vienna/Freiburg/Basel, 5th edition, 1962); see *The Mass of the Roman Rite* either ed. Benzinger Brothers, 1955 (reprinted by Four Courts Press, 1986), or revised edition, 1959.

3. A Latin/German bilingual peoples' missal [translator's note].

of non-liturgical forms of piety. It is against this contemporary background that the work of Pius Parsch should be understood and evaluated. In his time, he opened up for many people a new world, namely that of joining in together with the prayer and the sacrifice of the priest at the altar.

Unfortunately it is often that way with people: they swing from one extreme to the other. If, hitherto, the ritual accomplishment of the liturgical actions or of the sacrament by the priest, against a background of largely passive faithful, had dominated the scene, now the activity of the participants was overemphasised, and the cultic element, at the same time, was pushed into the background. [4] Pius Parsch's "Praying and Singing Mass" was often transformed into a prayer spoken by priest and people in alternation, and enlivened by a few hymns. Hardly a trace remained of the celebration of a mystery.

Today they go even further. Most forms of worship previously in use are despised by pastors and set aside as obsolete. No-one wants to give the impression of having missed-out on joining in modern developments. And yet the great mass of churchgoers is attached to these old forms, and their spirituality is based on them. Too little account is taken, by the over-zealous reformers of the present day, of how very much Catholic teaching, in the consciousness of the faithful, is identified with the particular forms of religious piety. For many of them, a change in the accustomed forms means a change in the teachings.

The development of Islam in Turkey shows clearly what dangers threaten here. When, after the First World War, at the instigation of the state, people began to dispense with old traditions which were based on the teaching of Mohammed, few had any idea of the effect these reforms would have on the religious attitudes of the masses. Contrary to what has happened in other Islamic countries, in which there was no such process of liberalisation, mosques in Turkey are for the most part empty nowadays, and hardly anyone answers the muezzin's call to prayer.

---

4. More on this point in the chapter "Actuosa Participatio" below.

Experience shows that people's involvement with religion is inseparable from the use of agreed forms of worship. If you destroy these, then you often destroy people's (last) link with God. That should have been taken into account by the modern reformers, who are unfortunately no psychologists. It is unfortunately the case: the religious practice of the masses consists above all in the observance of certain rules and customs. There are few who grasp the genuine content of religion. Is the Liturgy, then, meant only for this small minority?

It would certainly be mistaken, for example, to do away with the solemn "Rorate Office" in Advent, or the offertory procession in a requiem Mass, in some little mountain village, and to replace them with new forms which are alien to those people's cultural sensibilities. It would equally be quite wrong to despoil God's house of its accustomed ornamentation, against the will of the majority of the parishioners, and to want to re-order it in accordance with "the latest liturgical knowledge."

Upon how uncertain a footing this latest knowledge sometimes rests! We will come back to that. What is seen as modern today may already be old-fashioned tomorrow. And things are altered again. A permanent state of change, to the detriment of pastoral care!

We shouldn't deceive ourselves: changes in the prayers and the ritual do not automatically mean a more complete spiritual involvement on the part of the faithful. Our experience so far is hardly encouraging. Above all, the missionary power which ought to be imparted by our worship, and which in earlier times, above all in the early Church, was indeed thus imparted, seems now to be lacking.

For fifty years now the Orthodox Church in Russia has survived almost exclusively by the power of the Liturgy, though certainly in that country, more than almost anywhere else, it is deeply rooted in popular devotion, far more than has ever been the case in places where the Latin Liturgy was in use. The solemn celebration of the Liturgy, which is still carried out strictly in accordance with the traditional ceremonies and forms of prayer, now over a thousand years old, is the only "public activity" which the state permits the Russian clergy to undertake.

We ought first to think of that, when we hear about innovations: are they a help in pastoral care, or do they correspond only to an itch for novelty? Above all, however, we will not abandon the old forms, where they are good and have stood the test, unless there are good reasons for doing so, and especially not in favour of fashionable foolishness. But we will keep an open mind for new forms, if they really are better than the old, that is to say if they contribute to the "growth of the body (of the Church)" and to the "building up in love" (cf. Ephesians 4:16).

Amongst the current reforms, we must reckon as being entirely positive the greater emphasis on readings from Scripture, as well as a better choice of them,[5] and likewise the intercessions at the end of the Liturgy of the Word. The new Eucharistic prayers are also an enormous step forward, even if they are by no means to be regarded as ideal. In the same way, there are entirely positive aspects to the use of the vernacular. It would surely be wrong to use only the vernacular.

The penitential celebration at the beginning, which is taken from the rite of the Old Catholics, may be pastorally helpful, especially if it is not allowed to become merely an empty formula. Only it should be more clearly separated from the celebration of the Mass, to which, strictly speaking, it does not belong. The "prayers at the foot of the altar," which only became customary in the Roman rite in the later Middle Ages, and which are the starting-point for this development, did not represent a rite of penitence for the congregation. They constitute rather the act of preparation of the celebrant and his servers in view of the holy ritual about to begin. On this account they, like other private prayers, were spoken only quietly, while the choir was singing the introit. The so-called "Dialogue Mass" was the

---

5. The selection of Gospel pericopes in the new lectionary leaves much to be desired. Those who put it together seem to have been bereft of any knowledge of the various western and eastern Pericope systems. At least they made no use of them.

first in which the prayers at the foot of the altar were turned into a dialogue between priest and people.

But alongside these new forms of worship – the "modern rite" as we prefer to call it – the "Roman rite" which was laid down in the *Missale Romanum* of Pius V, and which is well over one thousand years old, should continue to be celebrated, at least for the time being. We will come back to that later.

In all attempts at reform, as we have already suggested, what is important is pastoral awareness, that is to say, a psychological sensitivity towards the degree of openness of the parish in question. What is good and acceptable in one parish may do harm in another. The main concern of liturgical renewal should not be the rapid application of given liturgical reforms, but a strengthening in the faithful of their capacity for spiritual participation in the performance of the sacred action. Only if this is successful is there any sense at all to changes made in the rite. All that is happening otherwise is that an old rite, which despite many weaknesses has stood the test of centuries, is replaced by a new one which is yet to be tested.

The Sacrifice of the Mass Since When?[1]

One of the problems at the heart of the reshaping of the Liturgy is the question as to the essential nature of the Mass;[2] for only if it is based on an understanding of its essential nature is it possible to construct a corresponding ritual structure. If the Mass is primarily a *meal*, then the rite will be different to the way it is if we are dealing with a *sacrifice* (with a concluding meal). Thus, for instance, in the first case the altar is simply a supper-table, in the second it is a sacrificial altar and should be arranged accordingly. The position which the priest takes up at the altar is also determined by this question. More about that later!

Whether, and in that case to what extent, the Mass is a sacrifice, is a problem which occupies people more than ever today. As in the time of the Reformers, people refer to what is said in the New Testament. This seems to have nothing to do with a ritual sacrifice. Thus, when Paul in the Letter to the Romans (12:1) says: "Offer your living bodies as a holy sacrifice, truly pleasing to God. (Thus you offer him) holy worship." Or when the Letter to the Hebrews emphasises the unique and exclusive character of the sacrifice of Jesus: "(Christ) had offered a single sacrifice, and he sat down for all time at the right hand of God...By a single offering, he has perfected for all time those who have been sanctified...Where there is forgiveness of these (sins), there is no longer any need of offering for sin" (10:12, 14, 18).

Yet if we look more closely at the Letter to the Hebrews, it distinguishes various types of sacrifice: first

---

1. This first appeared as "Die Messe ein Opfer - seit wann?" in: *Klerusblatt* no. 50 (1970), pp. 120-121.
2. The word "Mass" means much the same as "sacrifice" (oblatio); cf. K. Gamber, *Missa Romensis, Beiträge zur frühen römischen Liturgie und zu den Anfängen des Missale Romanum* [Essays on the early Roman Liturgy and on the Beginnings of the *Missale Romanum*] (*Studia patristica et liturgica* no. 3, F. Pustet, Regensburg, 1970) pp. 176-183.

the "sin offering," mentioned above (10:18); this was presented by Jesus, "offered without blemish" on the Cross to the Father (9:14), and is unique. It also talks at length about the "faithful service in God's house" (3:2) which, since his resurrection, Christ as the great high priest performs in heaven (4:15 – 5:10; 8:1-9, 28).

Towards the end of the same Letter to the Hebrews, it refers to another sacrifice which has its own altar: "We have our own altar, from which those who serve the tent have no right to eat...Through him (Christ) let us continually offer up to God a sacrifice of praise, the fruit of lips which acknowledge his name (cf. Psalm 50:14). Do not neglect to do good, nor the "Koinonia;" for such sacrifices are pleasing to God" (13:10, 15-16).

If this is a reference to an earthly "altar," at which only the faithful "may eat" (13:10), then to all appearances this can only be the "Lord's table" which Paul talks about (I Corinthians 10:21), and which he compares to pagan sacrificial meals. Paul quite clearly has the passage Malachi 1:12 in mind, where the altar in Jerusalem is similarly referred to as "the Lord's table." Sharing at the "altar" or at "the Lord's table" accordingly presupposes a sacrifice.

According to the Letter to the Hebrews, the sacrifice of the Church is above all a sacrifice of praise (13:10). Philo, in *De specialibus legis* I, 297, similarly calls thanksgiving a sacrifice. According to the writings of Qumran, too, "the sacrifice of the lips is the true thing like the sacrificial fragrance of righteousness" (the *Manual of Discipline*, I QS 9:4f.). The oldest prayers of the Roman Mass, including the Canon, refer to a "sacrifice of praise" [sacrificium laudis]; and this term appears again and again as a term for the Mass in the writings of the western Fathers, above all in Paulinus of Nola (†431).[3]

The Letter to the Hebrews, besides the once and for all sacrifice of Jesus and his everlasting service as High Priest in Heaven, and besides the sacrifice of praise of the congregation here on earth, talks about "doing good and the 'Koinonia'" as being sacrifices which are well pleasing

---

3. Cf. *Missa Romensis*, loc. cit., p. 182.

16

to God. The passage is not entirely clear. By 'Koinonia' (Communio) it seems to mean the celebration of the "Lord's Supper" (I Corinthians 11:20), and by "doing good" the gifts for those members of the community who are in need, which have been brought as gifts to this Agape/Eucharist. Paul calls these gifts a "service of the Liturgy" (II Corinthians 9:12). The expression is also to be found in the Acts of the Apostles, and indeed just where it speaks of the earliest congregation "Breaking Bread" in their own houses.[4]

Both Clement of Rome (around AD 96) and the author of the Letter of Barnabas (before AD 140) are decisively influenced by the intellectual environment of the Letter to the Hebrews, "the rôle of which in the development of the early Christian understanding of the Lord's Supper," as J. Betz rightly says,[5] "has certainly been underestimated by scholars." In his letter to the community at Corinth, Clement makes the point very strongly that there is a God-given order as to how the offerings (Greek, "Prosphorai") and the sacrificial worship (Greek, "Leitourgia") are to be carried out (I Clement 40:2,4). By "gifts" it seems most probable that here, as is later the case in Irenaeus' writings, the eucharistic gifts of bread and wine are meant.

Clement further speaks of Jesus as the "High Priest of our sacrificial offerings" (36:1). It is clear from this, that he sees no contradiction between the bishop making an offering on earth, and the high-priestly office of Jesus in Heaven, concerning which, as we have said, the Letter to the Hebrews talks at length.

---

4. Cf. K. Gamber, *Liturgie übermorgen. Gedanken über die Geschichte und Zukunft des Gottesdienstes* [Liturgy the day after tomorrow. Reflections on the History and the Future of Worship] (Herder, Freiburg, 1966) p. 27f.

5. J. Betz, "Die Prosphora in der patristischen Theologie" [The Prosphora in Patristic Theology], in: B. Neunhauser, *Opfer Christi und Opfer der Kirche* [The Sacrifice of Christ and the Sacrifice of the Church] (Düsseldorf, 1960), pp. 99-116; here p. 103. I have also made further use of this work by Betz. With regard to the early Middle Ages, see R. Schulte, *Die Messe als Opfer der Kirche. Die Lehre frühmittelalterliche Autoren über das eucharistische Opfer* [The Mass as the Sacrifice of the Church. The teaching of early mediaeval writers about the eucharistic sacrifice] *Liturgiewissenschaftliche Quellen und Forschungen* no. 35, Aschendorff, Münster-in-Westfalen 1959).

The Letter of Barnabas also connects to similar ideas when it calls Jesus' act of atonement an offering of his flesh for the redemption of sins (7:5), and specifically as a sacrifice (7:3). Like the Letter to the Hebrews, it speaks of the end of all hitherto existing sacrifices, both Jewish and pagan, and of a new sacrifice being set in their stead (2:6).

The Didache, probably the oldest extra-canonical Christian writing (around AD 100), quotes the prophet Malachi (1:11) as it specifically describes the celebration of Breaking Bread on the Lord's Day as a sacrifice (Greek, "Thusia"). The faithful must be reconciled with one another, that their sacrifice "may be pure" (14:1-3). Jesus' saying in Matthew 5:23f. forms the background for this, even if it is not directly referred to.

In the second century the material gifts of bread and wine are more definitely comprehended in the idea of sacrifice than hitherto. Thus Justin (around AD 150), once again with reference to Malachi 1:10-12, describes the bread and the cup of the Eucharist as the sacrificial gifts (Greek, "Thusiai") of the Christians (*Dialogue with Trypho*, 41:3).[6] But above all Irenaeus of Lyons (around AD 200), who in *Adversus Hæreses*, Book IV, 17:5 – 18:6, develops a doctrine of eucharistic sacrifice at some length, which may be regarded as corresponding to the ideas of the Church as a whole in the second century.

Because of its importance, we quote here the whole passage, with just a few passages omitted:

> He (Christ) advised his disciples to bring the first-fruits of creation to God, not as if he for his part had need of them, but in order that they might not be unfruitful. When therefore he took the gift of bread, he gave thanks and said: This is my body (Matthew 26:26). And similarly he confessed the cup, which springs from this earthly creation, to be his blood and made it the sacrificial gift of the New Covenant, so that the Church, as it has received the teaching from the Apostles, through all the world offers them to God…as the first-fruits of his gifts in the New Covenant.

---

6. Similarly in 117:1; cf *Bibliothek der Kirchenväter* (BKV) Justin, p. 62, also p. 189.

Amongst the Twelve Prophets, Malachi refers to this with the following words: I take no pleasure in you, says the Lord, the Almighty, and I find no sacrifice acceptable from your hands; for from the rising of the sun to its setting my name will be glorified amongst the nations, and in every place a sacrifice of incense will be offered to my Name, and a pure sacrifice, for my Name is great among the nations, says the Lord, the Almighty (Malachi 1:10-11)...

But this Name, which is to be glorified among the nations, is no other name but that of our Lord, through whom the Father is glorified... Since, then, the Name of the Son is also the Name of the Father, and since the Church brings its offering to almighty God through Jesus Christ, thus truly, and with a double reference, it says: And in every place a sacrifice of incense will be offered to my Name, and a pure offering. But John, in the Apocalypse (Revelation 5:8), refers to the prayers of the saints as a sacrifice of incense...

But the Lord wishes us to bring our sacrifice in all simplicity and innocence. Therefore he says with emphasis: If you are bringing your offering to the altar, and you remember that your brother has something against you, then leave your offering there before the altar, first go and be reconciled with your brother, and then come back and present your offering (Matthew 5:23).

We should therefore bring sacrifice to the Lord of creation, as Moses says: You shall not appear empty-handed before the face of the Lord your God (Deuteronomy 16:16)...We have not, therefore, rejected sacrifice,...only the kind and the manner of offering sacrifice have changed. For no longer are these offerings presented by slaves, but by children...

Because the Church brings its sacrifice in all simplicity, then its offering is rightly seen by God as a pure sacrifice...and only the Church can make this pure sacrifice to the Creator, by offering him with thanksgiving some of the creatures he has made...For we offer him from what is his own, by proclaiming the appropriate unity of flesh

19

and spirit. For just as the bread which is sprung from the earth, when it has received the Epiklesis of God, is no longer ordinary bread, but is the Eucharist, which consists of two elements, an earthly one and a heavenly, so also our bodies, when we have received the Eucharist, no longer belong to corruption, but now have the hope of resurrection.

We do not therefore make him offerings because he has need of them, but so as to thank his great majesty and to sanctify his gifts…He demands of us, that continually and without ceasing we bring him sacrifice at the altar. But the true altar is in heaven, whither our offerings and our prayers are directed, and the temple of which John says: And the temple of God in heaven was opened, and the tabernacle (Revelation 11:19). Behold, he says, here is the tabernacle of God, wherein he will dwell among men (Rev. 21:3)." (BKV Irenaeus vol. II, pp. 53-59)

One should read through these reflections of Irenaeus several times, in order to become familiar with every aspect of them. He says here, that at the Last Supper itself Jesus made bread and wine the sacrificial gifts of the New Covenant. It is thus that these gifts became the sacrifice of the Church, "its own sacrifice" which it presents to God through Christ. This is the "pure offering" which was predicted by Malachi. It is to be presented without cease at the altars. Its performance requires reconciliation with one's brother beforehand: thus, the same ideas as we have already seen in the Didache.

Irenaeus' teaching about the sacrifice of the Mass is largely in agreement with the early liturgical witnesses, above all with the Canon of the Roman Mass,[7] where at the beginning it says: "Uti accepta habeas et benedicas hæc dona…quæ tibi offerimus." To sacrifice means here, as in Irenaeus, quite simply: to bring something to God in thankfulness, by laying it upon the altar, which corresponds to the original meaning of the word "offerre."

---

7. With regard to the original form of the Canon of the Roman Mass, cf. *Missa Romensis* pp. 56-84.

The post-consecration prayer speaks about sacrificing to God what is already his ("offerimus…de tuis donis ac datis");[8] and the prayer asks that our offering be taken up onto the heavenly altar ("in sublime altare tuum in conspectu divinæ maiestatis tuæ"). Irenaeus too explains that we offer to God what is already his, and furthermore he talks about the true altar being in heaven, whither our prayers and our offerings are directed. Here the Letter to the Hebrews is clearly influencing him, with its emphasis on Christ's exercise of the office of High Priest in heaven, but above all ideas from the Book of Revelation.

The idea that, with regard to the command of Jesus (I Corinthians 11:24), we celebrate here the memorial of the Lord, above all of his death and his resurrection (cf. the Canon "memores…offerrimus") is actually lacking in this passage from Irenaeus, but is made explicit by Cyprian, who writes around AD 250 in Letter no. 63:17 (BKV Cyprian vol. II, p. 268): "In all our sacrifices we institute a memorial of his suffering."

In the writings of Cyprian, "oblatio" and "sacrificium" (with the qualification "dominicum") become the most prevalent terms in which he refers to the celebration of the Eucharist.[9] In his view, Christ too offered a sacrifice at the Last Supper ("Christus obtulit sacrificium"), "and indeed the same as that offered by Melchisedech, that is to say, bread and wine, in point of fact his body and his blood" (Letter 63:4; BKV Cyprian vol. II, p. 257). Cyprian is thereby expressing a similar idea to that of Irenaeus, who declares that Jesus has made the cup "the sacrificial offering of the New Covenant" (*Adversus Hæreses* Book IV, 17:5). Both these Fathers refer to the word spoken over the cup, which mentions the "blood of the New Covenant," "which is poured out for many for the forgiveness of sins" (Matthew 26:28). What is new in Cyprian's account is the reference to the sacrifice of Melchisedech, which also found its way into the Roman Canon.

---

8. Similarly in the Eastern liturgies, where it says, as in the Liturgy of St John Chrysostom: "We bring to you what is yours from what belongs to you: in all and for all."

9. Cf. *Missa Romensis* pp. 187-194.

When Cyprian, in Letter 63:17, after remarking, "In all sacrifices we institute a memorial of his passion," then adds, "for the passion of the Lord is the sacrifice which we offer," this is likewise a new idea. John Chrysostom says much the same thing; "Our High Priest has offered the purifying sacrifice (cf. Hebrews 10:18). And we now offer the same sacrifice" (Homilies on Hebrews, no. 17:3).

We find the transition to the mediaeval understanding of the sacrifice of the Mass in the writings of Gregory the Great (†604), who says, in *Dialogue* IV, 57-58 (BKV Gregory vol. II, p. 270f.):

This sacrifice saves us in a special way from eternal perdition, since in a mysterious manner it renews for us the death of the Incarnate One. For even though he has risen again and dies no more (Romans 6:9), yet in his immortal and incorruptible life he is offered anew for us in the mystery of the holy sacrifice, his Body is consumed in it, his flesh is shared out for the saving of the people, his blood is poured out...

Let us keep in mind, therefore, just what this sacrifice means for us, since for the sake of our redemption it ever anew presents the passion of the incarnate Son. For who amongst the faithful could doubt that in the hour of the sacrifice the heavens are opened at the voice of the priest, that the choirs of angels are present at this mystery, that above and below are then brought together, heaven and earth are united, the visible and the invisible become one?

But it is necessary that, whilst this holy transaction is being performed, we sacrifice God for ourselves in sorrowing contrition of heart (cf. Romans 12:1); for when we celebrate the mystery of the passion of the Lord, we must imitate what we are celebrating. Whenever we offer ourselves as a sacrifice, then the holy sacrifice which we present becomes truly a sacrifice on our behalf.

These foregoing expositions will have to suffice! They are intended above all to show one thing, that the idea of the Mass as a sacrifice is as old as the Church, even if it has undergone a certain transformation together with the Church. From the beginning, then, the Mass was both a meal and a sacrifice: a meal at which a sacrifice is offered to God through the Church.

In the Middle Ages, and right up to recent times, too much stress was laid on the idea of sacrifice, and the most diverse theories of the sacrifice of the Mass were constructed, without the appropriate lead having been taken from the Fathers and from the earlier liturgical texts; nowadays people lay stress above all on its aspect as a meal, and they shape their celebration of the Eucharist accordingly. Each of these one-sided attitudes is however wrong. The meal and the sacrifice belong together.

The aspect of the Mass as a meal is most apparent at the sharing of Communion, the sacrifice when the priest says the great Thanksgiving prayer. In the liturgical books of the East, this bears the name of "anaphora" (sacrificial prayer), whilst in those of the West the corresponding name is "Immolatio (missæ)," "Illatio" and "Prex (oblationis)."[10] It is in the course of this prayer that the "sacrificium laudis" is offered, with its thanks for our redemption and our election by Christ,[11] as well as the offering of the gifts of bread and wine being made, but above all, in fulfilment of Jesus' command, the remembrance of the Lord and the consecration of the bread and wine.

There was quite certainly no distortion in the development, even if in the course of time other aspects of the celebration of Mass became subordinated to the idea of sacrifice, as happened above all in the Eastern Church, a development whereby the celebration of the Eucharist turned more and more into a ritual performance.[12] It was wrong, on the other hand, when in the course of this development, both in the East and in the West, the aspect of the Mass as a meal was largely pushed into the background. It was not, however, the ritual itself which was responsible for this, but quite different factors, such as misunderstood rules concerning purity, and above all the half-heartedness of the faithful.

---

10. Cf. ibid., pp. 56-58.
11. Cf. *Liturgie übermorgen* p. 39ff.
12. Cf. ibid., p. 163ff.

THE MODERN RITE

Today we have, as in other matters, swung from one extreme to the other: from an overemphasis on the cultic aspect to an overemphasis of the aspect of the Mass as a meal. Already, more and more voices may be heard, calling, against all the tradition, to have the ritual, cultic element removed altogether from our worship.

Celebration
"Turned Towards the People"[1]

In his "Guidelines for the Layout and Arrangements of a Church in the Spirit of the Roman Liturgy," in 1949, Theodor Klauser says (no. 8) that:

There are many indications that in church buildings of the future the priest will once more stand behind the altar, as he did formerly, and will celebrate Mass facing towards the people, just as is still done in the Roman basilicas; the desire, which is felt everywhere, to have the eucharistic fellowship more clearly expressed by gathering round the table, seems to favour this solution.

What Klauser, in his day, posited as a desirable development, has in the meantime become widely regarded as the norm. People are almost all of the opinion that they have thereby restored an early Christian custom. But is this in fact really so?

In the following pages it will be shown that there never was a custom in the Church of celebrating "turned towards the people." The idea of priest and people facing one another during the Mass goes back without doubt to Martin Luther. In his little book "A German Mass and the Ordering of Worship," of 1526, at the beginning of the chapter "On Sunday for the Laity," he writes:

We allow the Mass vestments, altar and candles to remain, until they have been used up or until we decide to alter things. But if anyone wishes to do otherwise in this, then we permit it. But in the rightly celebrated Mass with only Christians in the congregation the altar ought not to remain

1. First appeared in: *Anzeiger für die katholische Geistlichkeit* [Catholic Clergy Gazette] no. 79 (1970) pp. 355-359; reprinted in: *Die Entscheidung. Blätter katholischen Lebens* [The Decision. Catholic Life Press] no. 14, September 1970, pp. 10-11; and in: *Una Voce - Korrespondenz* no. 1 (1970/71) pp. 102-108.

like that, and the priest should always turn towards the people, just as without doubt Christ did at the Last Supper. Well, that will come in its time.

In support of the change made in the way the priest stands at the altar, the reformer refers to what Christ did at the Last Supper. It seems that he had pictorial representations before him at that moment, such as were usual in his day: Jesus stands or sits in the middle of a large table, with the apostles to right and to left of him. The best-known picture of this kind is the painting by Leonardo da Vinci.

But did Jesus really take this particular place during the Last Supper? This is certainly not the case, for to do this would have been contrary to customary behaviour at table in the ancient world. In the time of Jesus, and for some centuries afterwards, people either used a round table or a sigma-shaped (semi-circular) one. The front of it was left free so that the food could be served. The diners sat or lay round the semicircle on the far side. They often made use of a sigma-shaped bench. The place of honour was not, as one might have thought, in the middle, but at the right-hand end (in cornu dextro).

We normally find this order of placing at table in the oldest depictions of Jesus at the Last Supper, right into the Middle Ages.[2] Jesus is always lying or sitting at the right-hand side of the table. Not until the thirteenth century and later does a new type of picture gradually become predominant: Jesus now has his place on the far side of the table, in the midst of the apostles. This does indeed look like a eucharistic celebration "turned towards the people." Yet in reality it was not so, since, as we all know, the "people" towards whom Jesus would have had to turn were not in fact present in the upper room at the Last Supper. This is the point which undermines Luther's argument.

In the first three or four centuries, when there were still relatively few people in the congregation, celebrations of the Eucharist still preserved the same order of

---

2. Cf. Klaus Wessel, *Abendmahl und Apostelkommunion* [The Supper and the Communion of the Apostles], Recklinghausen, 1964.

places at table, in faithful imitation of what was done at the Last Supper. Various house-churches which have been unearthed by archaeologists in the Alpine and Danube region show this quite clearly. Here, in each case, we find in the middle of a fairly small worship area (about 9 metres by 17) a stone bench, semi-circular in form, which will seat about twenty-five people. This has been discussed in detail in another study.[3]

In the towns, where there were a greater number of believers, it was necessary to put up several tables when the Eucharist was celebrated. At one of these the bishop and priest were seated, at others the men and the women. This grouping of those participating in the eucharistic supper appears in the *Didascalia Apostolorum* (Book II, 57:2 – 58:6) in the third century.[4]

In the next stage of development there are no longer any tables for the laity. Only the bishop's table remains. The table for the Lord's Supper, originally for the most part made of wood, now develops into a stone altar. In those places where hitherto all the believers sat at a single table, the room which at first had been small was extended because of the great increase in numbers of the congregation at the beginning of the fifth century. The worshippers now sat on benches set along the side-walls of the church building, a custom corresponding to that in the synagogues. These benches represent in fact an extension of the sigma-bench, on which henceforth only the bishop and the clergy took their places.

---

3. Cf. Klaus Gamber, *Domus ecclesiæ. Die ältesten Kirchenbauten Aquilejas sowie im Alpen- und Donaugebiet bis zum Beginn des 5. Jahrhundert liturgiegeschichtlich untersucht* [The House of the Church. An investigation in terms of the History of Worship of the oldest church buildings in Aquileia, together with those in the Alpine and Danube Regions, up to the beginning of the Fifth Century.] (Studia patristica et liturgica, vol. 2, Regensburg (Friedrich Pustet) 1968).

4. Cf. Gamber, "Die frühchristliche Hauskirche nach Didascalia Apostolorum II, 57:1 - 58:6" [The Early Christian House-Church according to *Didascalia Apostolorum* II, 57:1 - 58:6], in: *Studia Patristica X* (Texte und Untersuchingen, Berlin (W; de Gruyter) 1970), pp. 337-344.

A further question is this: when the celebrant went to the altar for the sacrificial rite, was he in front of it, or behind it? It would seem obvious for him to take the shortest way from his place in the middle of the bench, to the rear side of the altar and to take up position there. In this case there would therefore be a celebration "turned towards the people."

There were however, as we know, other quite different points of view which were determinative for the positioning of the priest at the altar, specifically the eastward alignment. The custom of turning towards the rising sun to pray is ancient.[5] The rising sun was seen as a symbol for the Lord going up to heaven, who would come again from thence. This idea is to be found in the *Didascalia Apostolorum*, to which we have already referred (II, 57:6): "Versus orientem oportet vos orare, sicut et scitis, quod scriptum est: Date laudem Deo qui ascendit in cælum cæli ad orientem" (Psalm 67:33-34).

In order to let the rays of the rising sun stream into the inside of the church during the celebration, in most Western basilicas of the fourth century the entrance was not made in the west, as was later customary everywhere, but in the east. This can still be recognised in the principal churches of Rome. The three entrance doors had to be left open during the service, as will be readily understood, so as to let the sunlight in.

In order for the celebrant to be able to face east during the holy sacrifice, in a basilica arranged in that wise, he had to stand behind the altar. The result thus appeared to be a celebration "turned towards the people." Yet we must not forget that those believers who were present were not, as is frequently believed, standing in the middle of the nave, but were in the two side-aisles, and likewise turned

---

5. Cf. Franz J. Dölger, *Gebet und Gesang im christlichen Altertum mit besonderer Rücksicht auf die Ostung in Gebet und Liturgie* [Prayer and Song in Christian Antiquity, especially with respect to Orientation in Prayer and Liturgie; normally referred to by its principal title, *Sol Salutis*] (*Liturgiegeschichtliche Forschungen*, H. 4-5, 1st edition 1920, 2nd edition 1925).

to look towards the east. In the Egyptian Liturgy of Saint Mark there is even a point where the Deacon cries, appropriately: "Look to the East!" In the west-aligned basilicas of the fourth century, then, the congregation who had met for the celebration of the holy sacrifice used to stand in a semicircle which was open towards the east. The apex of this semicircle was represented by the celebrating bishop (or, in some cases, priest). Here, too, is the semicircle, just as when people sat on a stone bench during the celebration of the primitive Christian "Lord's Supper!"

Thus, during the sacrificial rite in the basilicas of the fourth century the priest and people did not stand facing one another. This has been overlooked by the Liturgical Movement of the twenties and thirties, who popularised the idea of a celebration "turned towards the people," just as Luther had done. Thus Pius Parsch, deserving of all praise as a congregational liturgist, as early as when the little church of Saint Gertrude in Klosterneuburg was re-ordered in the nineteen-thirties, had the altar arranged for a celebration "turned towards the people."

Accordingly, the position of the priest between the apse and the altar in those fourth-century basilicas we have mentioned was determined solely by the custom of praying "ad orientem." Thence the question as to how long celebration "turned towards the people" remained customary, which is dealt with by Nußbaum in his great work "The position of the Liturgical Leader at the Christian Altar up to the Year 1000,"[6] is not in this form correctly expressed.

When in the fifth century they started to align not the entrance, but the apse, to the east, the position of the priest at the altar had consequently to change. From now on he stood with his back to the congregation, turned towards the apse. Jungmann remarks, about this: "Thus the priest stands at the head of the people, not 'turned towards the people.' The entire congregation is like a great procession,

---

6. O. Nußbaum, "Der Standort des Liturgen am christlichen Altar vor dem Jahre 1000. Eine archäologische und liturgiegeschichtliche Untersuchung" [The Position...to the Year 1000. An Investigation from the points of view of Archaeology and of the History of Liturgy] (*Theophaneia* no. 18, vols. 1-2, Bonn 1965).

which, led by the priest, might be moving to the east, towards the sun, to meet Christ the Lord, so as to offer the sacrifice to God with him."[7]

The relationships are somewhat different in some early churches in North Africa and northern Italy, as for instance at Ravenna. In these the apse is indeed at the eastern end, yet the altar is placed not in the apse but almost exactly in the middle of the church. The faithful took their place in the side-aisles, as in other basilicas, which corresponds to the sitting on benches along the sides of smaller hall-churches.

Since the celebrant, when standing at the altar, turned towards the east, that is, towards the apse, in these churches he was not standing at the head of the people; he represented rather, similarly to what was the case in the west-aligned basilicas of the fourth century, the apex of a great semicircle of the faithful sharing in the sacrifice, a semicircle open towards the east.

Here we must meet an objection, the assertion that in fact, as Klauser says and, following him, Nußbaum, at an early stage "the altar, as the place of theophany, became at the same time the point towards which worship was oriented" and that thus the obvious thing to do was "to turn towards the altar, even if in so doing the liturgical leader, in a church with the apse at the east, was facing towards the west."[8]

Nußbaum further remarks that in those cases where there was room enough for the priest conducting the celebration between the altar and the wall of the apse, or, as the case might be, the bishop's throne, then we may conclude that the priest, too, had his own place here and was thus looking "towards the people" when he stood at the altar.

Here, modern conceptions are being projected back into an early period. There is for instance not a single lit-

---

7. J.A. Jungmann, *Liturgie der christlichen Frühzeit* [English trans. "The Early Liturgy to the time of Gregory the Great," Indiana (Notre Dame University Press) 1959] (Freiburg in der Schweiz, 1967) p. 126.

8. Cf. Nußbaum, "Der Standort des Liturgen am christlichen Altar," p. 403.

erary witness which goes beyond the special symbolism of the altar and names it as the point of orientation. The archaeological witnesses to which Nußbaum appeals are by no means unambiguous and do not constitute evidence for a celebration "turned towards the people."

In any case, the practice of precisely aligning churches with the east, which we find from the 4th/5th century onwards, would have been quite meaningless, if it had no connection with the direction in which people turned to pray. We can state as a general rule: If a church is aligned with its apse towards the east, then the priest had his place "before the altar," so that he could look towards the east while offering the holy sacrifice.

The idea of the priest standing facing the congregation during the celebration of Mass is therefore nowhere to be found in literary sources before the time of Luther, and nor can the archaeological evidence be called in support of this conception.[9]

The particular expression "towards the people," "versus populum," is first to be found in the "Ritus servandus in celebratione Missæ," in the *Missale Romanum* which was published in 1570 at the behest of Pope Pius V. This (in section V, 3) deals with the case in which "the altar is turned towards the east, (yet not towards the apse, but) towards the people" (altare sit ad orientem, versus populum), which, as is well known, corresponds to the layout of the principle churches in Rome and of some of the other old churches in that city.

But the emphasis here is on "ad orientem," whilst "versus populum" is merely an explanatory remark, with

---

9. Martin Luther's suggestion was taken up only occasionally here and there in Protestant churches, above all by Reformed congregations; cf. Fr. Schulz, "Das Mahl der Brüder" [The Supper of the Brethren], in: *Jahrbuch für Liturgik und Hymnologie*, vol. 15 (1970) p. 34, note 18, which refers to the fact that Martin Bucer, during his time in Strassburg, had the table set up for the Lord's Supper "so that the minister turns his face towards the people," and that in the Wittenberg *Order of Ceremonies* from the year 1668 it was supposed to be the case that, at the Lord's Supper, the minister had the altar and the people in front of him, unless it were that the altar was fixed to the back wall of the church.

reference to the direction immediately afterwards, that the celebrant should not turn round (non vertit humeros ad altare) for "Dominus vobiscum," seeing that he is already turned "ad populum."

How are things arranged in the Eastern Church? Here too there was never a time when a celebration "turned towards the people" was customary, since there is no explicit witness to it. It is remarkable that in the case of a concelebration, of which there is a long tradition in the Eastern Church, the principal celebrant normally stands with his back to the congregation, while the priests who are concelebrating stand to his right and his left. But at no point do they take up a position behind the altar.

The decisive question, with regard to the position of the priest at the altar, is, as we have already mentioned several times, the character of the Mass as a sacrifice. The person offering the sacrifice turns towards the person to whom the sacrifice is being presented. By early Christian conceptions, one did this by turning to look towards the east.

It is well known that Luther denied that the Mass has the character of a sacrifice. Various modern Catholic theologians and liturgists do not actually deny the sacrificial aspect of the Mass, but would prefer nonetheless to leave it more in the background and to give greater emphasis to the aspect of the Mass as a meal. This is often done from ecumenical motives, with respect to Protestants, whilst any similar consideration towards the Eastern Church is ignored.

The aspect of the Mass as a sacrifice and its aspect as a meal have never, in the Catholic view, stood in opposition to one another. The meal and the sacrifice are two elements of the same celebration. It is certainly true, that in the course of history these two elements have not always been equally apparent. Thus, the aspect of the Mass as a meal was clearly dominant during the first three centuries, and found expression in the custom of sitting together at the same Supper Table. Besides this, the Eucharist and the Love Feast were still closely associated with each other at that period. The "Breaking of Bread" on a Sunday was nevertheless explicitly referred to as a sacrifice by the *Didache* (14:2) in about the year A.D. 100.

If nowadays people wish to lay more emphasis on the aspect of the Mass as a meal, this is not made so clear by means of celebrating "turned towards the people," as many people both believe and wish to be the case. When this is done, only the "Meal Leader" himself actually takes his place at the table. Since the rest of those taking part in the meal sit down in the nave, that is to say in "the audience," they have no direct relationship with the Supper Table.

One can best do justice to the aspect of the Mass as a sacrifice if, during the Eucharistic Prayer, in the course of which the holy sacrifice is consummated, all the people together with the priest turn in the same direction (that is to say, towards the east). The aspect of a meal, in turn, could be brought out more clearly by the way the ritual of Communion is shaped. We do not need to give any particular explanation here why it is that priest and readers should face the people for the proclamation of the Word of God.

According to the Catholic conception of the Mass, it is more than just a communal meal in memory of Jesus of Nazareth. The decisive element is not the way that the community spirit is made effective and experienced, even though that should not be underestimated (cf. I Corinthians 10:17), but the community coming to offer service to God. The point of reference must always be God, and not man.[10] For that reason, from the outset, the turning towards him in prayer by all those present and no turning to face each other by priest and people. We must draw the necessary conclusions and see the celebration "turned towards the people" for what it really is, an invention of Martin Luther.

Postscript: O. Nußbaum has criticised my exposition in: *Zeitschrift für katholische Theologie,* no. 93 (1971), pp. 148-167. Yet he has not succeeded in refuting my theses, but has merely effected a few minor corrections. I will answer him fully elsewhere. Worthy of notice is the essay of M. Metzger, "La place des liturges à l'autel," in: *Revue des sciences religieuses* no. 45 (1971), pp. 113-145, where the book by Nußbaum which has several times been cited is discussed in detail and my own view is to a great extent substantiated, without the writer's having read my article. In conclusion, indeed, he makes suggestions very similar to my own, when he says: "Les positions du liturge pourraient être les suivantes: se tourner vers l'assemblée lorsqu'il s'addresse à elle, c'est-à-dire lors des salutations...lorsqu'il annonce la Parole de Dieu et lors de la distribution de la communion; se tourner vers l'abside pour toutes les prières." [The liturgical leader might take up the following positions: turning towards the congregation when he is addressing them, that is for the greetings...when he is proclaiming the Word of God, and for the Communion; turning towards the apse for all the prayers.] (p. 143).

---

10. Cf. on this point what is said by K.G. Rey in his publication *Pubertätserscheinungen in der katholischen Kirche* [Manifestations of Puberty in the Catholic Church] (*Kritische Texte Benzinger* [Critical Texts, published by Benzinger] no. 4): "Whilst hitherto the priest, as an anonymous intermediary, as the foremost member of the congregation, turned towards God and not towards the people, offered the sacrifice as a representative for everyone and together with everyone, whilst the prayers he had to say...were prescribed for him, he now stands up as a person, with his own personal peculiarities, his personal life-style and turns his face towards us. For many of them this means a temptation to prostitute their own person, a temptation they are not sufficiently mature to resist. On the contrary! Many of them learn how, in a refined way - sometimes not such a refined way - they can turn this to their own advantage. Their gestures, their silent miming and the attitudes they strike, their entire behaviour becomes a suggestive, eye-catching way of directing attention to their own person. Many of them, in addition to this, forcibly draw attention to themselves by repeated remarks, directions, and most recently by means of personal forms of greeting and farewell...The degree of success of their suggestive behaviour is for them the measure of their power and thereby the norm of their security" (p. 25).

The Problem of the Vernacular[1]

The difficulties involved in the current reform of the Liturgy are revealed above all in the almost exclusive use of the vernacular language of each country in the celebration of the Holy Mass. From a pastoral perspective it would be most foolish to dispute the right to make use of the vernacular. It is merely a question of the extent to which it is used in worship. Before any attempt at a solution to this problem, we may notice what is said by a few people who express their views on this in the Norwegian newspaper "Farmand," which is not normally accessible to us.[2]

In a communication from a correspondent which appeared in issue no. 14, of the 2nd April 1966, we read:

There can be no doubt of the rising tide of astonishment amongst Catholic laypeople, at the liturgical changes and the new forms which are following in the wake of the Vatican Council. The Council did not order the removal of Latin from the Liturgy, the Decree on the Liturgy even says (in no. 36) the opposite, to wit that Latin should be retained in the Roman rite, but at the same time a more or less widespread introduction of the vernacular in the Mass should be permitted, where this "will benefit the people." In no. 54 of the decree it is recommended that the faithful should be capable of saying and singing those parts of the Liturgy in Latin, where the people join in the words. This is a clear expression in favour of the coexistence of the Latin and the vernacular forms. But in practice we see a one-sided tendency to suppress the Latin.

The Liturgy has an effect on Christians' daily lives, and in the present situation many Catholics have become aware

---

1. First appeared under the title "Zur Problematik der gegenwärtigen Liturgiereform" [On the Difficulties in the Current Reform of the Liturgy] in *Heiliger Dienst* no. 23 (1969) pp. 6-10; here it has been extensively reworked.

2. For the translation of the following passages I am indebted to the friendly help of Fräulein Helmtrud Schmitt, of Munich.

– if they were not already aware – that the Latin form was not so incomprehensible and impenetrable, but that it gave their religious life living nourishment and fruitfulness. Everywhere there are groups of laypeople who have asked the authorities to be allowed to keep the Latin form side-by-side with the vernacular one. But this is where the astonishment arises, for the reaction to these requests has all too frequently been either a disapproving silence or a direct prohibition of any discussion of the subject. This is despite the fact that this desire is perfectly legitimate so far as the Decree on Liturgy of the Vatican Council is concerned…

In no. 17 of the same periodical, published on the 23rd April 1966, another similar communication says:

The introduction of the vernacular is really due to a misunderstanding, and is the sign of a really provincial mentality. Perhaps it might have been appropriate, two hundred years ago, and it was a tragedy for the Church in the Far East, when Jansenist conspirators in Rome prevented the Jesuits from introducing an East Asian rite. But today we live in a world in which millions of tourists are forever travelling all round the globe, in which millions of workers go to work in other countries, in which hundreds of thousands of businessmen travel from one country to another, in which distances have been abolished by jet fighters. By tomorrow everywhere will be part of one single Babel.

The Spanish worker who went into a Catholic Church in the Ruhr used to hear a language he knew. Not any longer! I used to be able to travel to every land under the sun, and with my little mass-book I could read the Mass at the same time as the priest. Not any longer! When, a few months ago, I was in Saigon, and was about to go into the cathedral, a young man said to me: "Monsieur, your Mass is not until ten o'clock." "I'm sorry," I replied in French, "but I have to go to Mass now." I listened fascinated to a Mass which was proclaimed with strange sounds in a monosyllabic language, but I could not join in the prayers. Later I was talking with a refugee from Tonkin: "I too did not enjoy the Mass. You know, the priest had a dreadful Cochin-china accent!"

Nairobi. What is the "vernacular" in Nairobi? More than a third of the congregation speak Konkani. The official language is English. The "universal" language is Swahili. The language of the streets is Kikuyu, Luo and a bit of Masai...And what is supposed to happen in ethnically mixed areas, where there is enmity between different groups: Belgium (possibly with demonstrations in Church), South Tyrol, the Basque country...and above all in India, where a few years ago thousands of people were killed in disturbances about language?

And besides that: modern people "see" more than they "hear"...Furthermore: all great religions have a sacred language. Mohammedans have classical Arabic, Buddhists Pali, Hindus Sanskrit and the Greek Catholic Church has old Greek and Church Slavonic...

Finally, a few sentences from a letter to the editor:

What kind of experiments have we yet to face? Will we never again be at peace? I am anxious above all about the amount of freedom which is going to be allowed to individual celebrants...Their hatred of Latin is now satisfied. But now it's the old translations. They must be made "contemporary"...And then of course it will have to be changed every twenty years, since the language also changes. Professor Walter Frei, a Christian Catholic Swiss theologian, has written a disturbing article in the Lucerne Church paper, in which as an Old Catholic he absolutely deplores the step his Church has taken, and calls on us to avoid falling into the same trap of eradicating all trace of mystery and solemnity from our worship. They have not found that their churches were fuller as a result, rather the opposite...

So much for these voices, which we should not ignore. They are more numerous than we might like to think, and their number is steadily growing.

It has all happened before. 150 years ago, when there were similar aspirations to those of today, Michael Sailer (†1832), then Bishop of Regensburg, wrote the following admonition:

Worship has a fundamental language, a vernacular of its own, which is neither Latin nor German, neither Hebrew nor Greek, it is not, to be brief, a language of words at all...The life, the gestures, the comportment, glance, facial expression, the attitude of the person, in a word: the totality of expression of religion in the life and the entire visible person, that is the true basic language and vernacular of all worship. The word is certainly comprised within this basic vernacular. But the word is neither the whole, nor even the principal element of this language...Whoever wishes to reform public worship, therefore, must begin by training-up enlightened and spiritual priests...

It also seems as though many a spokesman for the rapid introduction of German has not yet become completely self-aware, otherwise his own reason would have told him: do not expect such great things from German...[3]

A critical observer would sometimes have the impression today that liturgical reform has become an end in itself, through which the bright ideas of just a few liturgists are put into practice, sometimes without consideration for the wishes or the needs of the faithful, above all those of older people who have been used to the previous forms of worship from the time of their youth.

Just as it is impossible to halt a development which as a whole is perfectly justified, so equally it would not be a good idea suddenly to give up using the previous forms of worship, which have been shaped by a long development, behind which there often stands a great deal of pastoral experience. Unfortunately, this is what has happened almost everywhere. There is hardly anywhere, today, that one can attend a solemn choral Mass in Latin.

After everything that has been said, there is one solution open today, which was envisaged in its essentials by the Constitution on the Liturgy: both forms, the old Latin Liturgy and a new one in the vernacular, could be in use side-by-side with equal privileges, that is to say that

---

3. Cf. Gamber, *Liturgie übermorgen* pp. 256-258.

both forms should be equally respected and used in each single parish. As to the detailed arrangements, we would suggest the following.

The two liturgical forms should be clearly separated from one another. The old Roman rite and the *Missale Romanum* should be restored in the form they had before about 1960, and should remain for the moment unchanged. The only exception would be the reading of lessons in the vernacular, which should be allowed "ad libitum," because there is a genuine concern behind this.

The changes in ritual of the last few years should be limited to worship in the national language; this would include the new lectionary, the intercessions before the offertory, the new Canons of Mass, the Our Father being said by the people, and the new rite for communion and dismissal. The new style of Eucharist would then not be privileged as the Roman rite, but would be in use as another rite "ad experimentum." Whether this will then be generally received, the future alone will show.

There is nothing to be gained by applying the current experiments to the traditional Roman rite itself, since in that way an important element of each of the celebrations would be lost: that of consistency. Yet if we leave the Roman rite unchanged and continue to celebrate it alongside the new forms, then on account of the Latin language in which it is celebrated another element, which could indeed be important for the future, will be preserved: the element of unity, which brings different peoples together: a concern which is too easily overlooked in the intoxication of reforming the Liturgy.

The strict separation to be maintained, as suggested here, between the Roman rite and the new vernacular Liturgy, the "ritus modernus," and the use of both forms of liturgy at the same time in individual churches, would solve many of the liturgical problems which are cropping-up today. Above all, this would meet the justifiable demands of many Catholics – there is talk of some 40% – who have been mentioned above, who argue for a retention of the old forms of worship, without neglecting the equally justifiable demands of the others for an up-to-date Liturgy. But it would be necessary for both forms to be given genuine parity in practice until further notice. Therefore, in larger parishes there would have to be a celebration of Latin High Mass every Sunday, and perhaps sometimes also a silent Holy Mass on weekdays or early on Sunday morning.

Whereas, finally, for the Roman rite the rubrics previously in force should continue to be valid – which state of affairs need not exclude minor alterations – with respect to the "ritus modernus" a great deal should be permitted "ad libitum" or "ad experimentum," and similarly a particular form could be developed in each country. In this way, the ancient, old-established form could be preserved, without barring the way for an organic development in the future.

Not long ago an experienced priest wrote much the same thing to the author:

> If, four hundred years ago, Pius V allowed older priests to continue to use their accustomed rite, ought Paul VI to be more rigorous and less humane than his saintly predecessor? With one "ad libitum" he could extend his help to an entire generation of older priests, for which he would be remembered with gratitude when he is long in his grave.

In the Roman Catholic Church today, one reform follows upon another. Whilst in the past the Curia allowed itself plenty of time to consider innovations – sometimes, far too long! – today these follow hard on each other's heels. It is as if people wanted to catch up, in just a few years, on all the missed opportunities of centuries. Amongst these reforms are some, like the permission to use the vernacular, which might once have brought great blessings, if they had only come earlier.

In the age of weak faith in which we live, voices are raised ever louder, urging us to save what can be saved. That means in our case, in concrete terms: the old Roman rite must be kept untouched, not only for older priests, but also as a sign of unity for Catholics all over the world, and as a fixed point of rest, in our restless world of constant change and reform; at least until we are able to create a new and truly ecumenical Liturgy (more on this in the final chapter).

Some Criticism
of the New *Ordo Missæ*[1]

Much of what has been promulgated by way of liturgical innovation during the past twelve years – beginning with the decree of the Sacred Congregation for Rites issued on September 3rd 1958, and the "new" code of rubrics of July 25th 1960, which has meanwhile been superseded, and passing, by way of constant small changes, to the reform of the *Ordo Missæ* of April 6th 1969 – has already proved to be unusable for the long term.

As regards the *Ordo Missæ*, Vatican II in the Constitution on the Sacred Liturgy, in section fifty, did indeed demand a reworking and expressed some ideas about it, yet without going into detail or setting any date. It says merely that the work should start "quam primum" (no. 25).

But hardly five years after Vatican II, work on the new *Ordo Missæ* had been completed and it was presented to the Pope for his approbation. The promulgation of the pattern exemplar – after a few changes, as we know – followed in the same authoritarian form in which, since the Council of Trent, the Congregation for Sacred Rites had always undertaken little changes to the official Roman rite. In the course of this procedure, a few of the fathers of the new rite of Mass seem to have quite knowingly availed themselves of the rubricism they attacked in their writings, so as to impose their own ideas.

Since then, opposition to the new *Ordo Missæ* within the Church has been growing. Even well-known cardinals have spoken out against it.[2] We can only offer criticism on a few points here.

---

1. First appeared in *Heiliger Dienst* no. 24 (1970) pp. 16-18; reprinted in: *Anzeiger für die katholische Geistlichkeit* no. 79 (1970) pp. 58-60; and in *Entscheidung* no. 12, May 1970, pp. 10-12.

2. [Cf. A. Ottaviani & A. Bacci, *The Ottaviani Intervention*, Tan, Rockford 1992.]

The most interesting thing seems to be: not only the conservatives, no, also even the so-called progressives are in no way content with the new Mass rite. The latter above all because some of their wishes have not been taken into account, and the whole thing then obviously represents an unfortunate compromise.

Those who count themselves among the progressives, above all the younger clergy, will hardly keep strictly to the rules of the new rite in the future. They will conduct further experiments. Thereby, the liturgical muddle will just increase still further. The conservatives, again, just don't understand the point of all these innovations, which disrupt an old tradition without putting anything new, still less anything better, in its place. From a sense of conscientious duty they will observe the new rubrics as best they can.

What is here presented as the new *Ordo Missæ* is by no means new. The similarity to the rite of the German-speaking Old Catholics is downright amazing; right from the "little penitential rite" at the beginning, passing through the form of the intercessions after the sermon, and the "Domine non sum dignus," now only spoken once, which has been assigned to the people even before the priest's Communion, right up to the "Go in Peace!" which only happens after the blessing from the celebrant.[3] These are sheer "modern achievements," which appeared in the Old Catholic rite, amongst other things, some ten years ago.

It is well known that the Old Catholic Church nowadays makes use of two forms of *Ordo Missæ*. These were introduced in 1960, that is, before Vatican II, by the then Bishop Demmel. They were however not well received in all local congregations. The leadership of the Church, however, does not compel any local congregation to introduce the new altar-books.

---

3. I have before me two little books: *Die Zelebration der heiligen Eucharistie, Die Zelebration der heiligen Eucharistie Erste Meßordnung, Zweite Meßordnung* [The celebration of the Holy Eucharist *First Order of Mass, Second Order of Mass*], published by Bruderschaft St. Andreas-Mission & Co., 8000 Munich 13, Türkenstraße 104/0.

Whilst, accordingly, the Old Catholic Eucharist may have served as a model to those who compiled the new *Ordo Missæ* – the agreements are all too obvious! – they seem to have made too many concessions to the Protestants, with respect to dogma, in the definition of the Mass in no. 7 of the "Institutio Generalis Missali Romani" which is prefaced to the Ordo. The Mass is here defined as "the Lord's Supper," as "the sacred congregation, the gathering together of the People of God to celebrate under the leadership of the priest the Remembrance of the Lord."[4]

Almost any believing Protestant, of whatever denomination, would be able to assent to such a definition. But this does not coincide with the teaching on the Mass of the Early Church or that of the Middle Ages, and still less with the dogmatic statements of the Council of Trent. In the Catholic view the Mass is more than just a "remembrance." It is at the same time the sacrifice of the New Covenant which was foretold by Malachi (cf. *Didache* ch. 14).[5]

The word sacrifice is deliberately avoided in the text of the "Institutio Generalis Missalis Romani." It appears only incidentally, as in no. 2 (sacrificium eucharisticum). The Constitution on the Sacred Liturgy, on the other hand, speaks repeatedly and quite clearly of the "sacrificium missæ" (thus in no. 49, and similarly no. 55), whilst now mention is made merely of "Eucharistia" (no. 282, no. 285) or of "celebratio eucharistica" (no. 5, no. 284).

It is not really credible that this is a matter of chance, it is rather the deliberate intention of a group of progressive liturgists to relegate to the background the sacrificial character of the Mass, and correspondingly to emphasise its quality as a meal. This is quite clear from the requirement laid down in no. 262 to separate the altar from the wall "so that one may more easily move round it, and may stand there to celebrate the Mass facing the congregation."

Let it be said yet again: in the early Church there

---

4. Quotation from the German translation appearing in *Heiliger Dienst* no. 23 (1969) p. 61 [and here translated directly from Gamber's quotation.]

5. In the new [1970] *Missale Romanum* this definition, which was a matter of dispute, has been changed.

was never a celebration turned towards the people, as it is understood today. Even if the altar was free of superstructure, and was free-standing in the presbytery – as it is today in the oriental rites – the priest always stood in front of the altar to celebrate the Eucharist, that is, with his back to the people.

We should further note that much has been included in the new *Ordo Missæ*, such as a part of the "ritus initiales," which is untried, and which is contrary to the previous customary attitude of the Sacred Congregation for Rites. And this untried material was immediately given a permanent place, even before it had proved its worth. The reason for this is that in the final analysis the reform has not yet gone far enough, and the authoritarian ways of thought and the habit of "lawgiving" have not been abandoned. That ought to have been the first aim of any reform. But apparently no-one had sufficient courage for this.

Instead of new rubrics, norms or guidelines ought to have been issued, which should have set definite limits to what was permissible, but within which the celebrant would have been allowed a certain degree of freedom in shaping the worship, as for instance in the choice of weekday readings or in the celebration of saints' days.

Above all, however, the new missal will prevent, for the foreseeable future, a genuine and lasting reform of worship, in the spirit of Vatican II. In my book "Liturgy the day after Tomorrow" I have set out in detail how the new rite might in my view be constituted.[6] In doing so, I laid deliberate emphasis on the point that such a reform is not possible at present, because of the lack of various necessary preconditions.

The new *Ordo Missæ* is like a minor eruption of a volcano, which immediately cools again and becomes petrified. What we urgently need in the Church today is much more a fluidity in our spiritual life, which would help to overcome the crisis of faith, which is at the same time a crisis of authority. Life does not exclude order and authority. It is only within an ordered environment that life, espe-

---

6. *Liturgie übermorgen*, especially p. 174ff. Cf. also the final chapter.

cially spiritual life, can flourish. It can even flourish in an order which at first glance might seem obsolete, such as the old rite. The new *Ordo Missæ* is really not what would have been needed in order to activate it in the present day.

We should also bear in mind that only a Church which is strong in faith and spiritually fruitful is capable of building something really new and lasting. Everything else is just a matter of artificial fabrication, often undertaken without reference to the real requirements of a modern and world-wide pastoral policy, but above all without any psychological sensitivity to the way of thinking of the people, or, it would be better to say, of the peoples and races upon earth.

If, in the future, new forms of rite were to crystallise in various countries, then we should welcome this. But one cannot then pour this new matter into old moulds, as has been done in the new missal. Here untried material has been given a permanent place, but without being able to prevent things running wild, indeed, this is even still being encouraged, at least indirectly.

Since there is at present still no solution in sight which would be generally satisfactory, the Church should retain the rite in use hitherto, and should provisionally permit *ad libitum* certain reforms motivated by pastoral concerns, which have already proved their worth, such as the readings in the vernacular and various other things. But on no account should they abrogate the old *Missale Romanum*, which at the moment is only being permitted for another two years. That would be a mistake which could hardly be retrieved, either at present or in the future.

On the Changes
to the Calendar of Saints[1]

When children finally find out that the Saint Nicholas who always came on the sixth of December is not at all
"genuine," they think they are being very clever. They do
not understand the deeper meaning of this custom, and do
not know that a holy bishop called Nicholas really lived
in Myra, and that since the eleventh century his grave is
to be found in Bari, and that miraculous healings beyond
number have happened there.

One cannot get rid of the impression that those
engaged in reforming the calendar at present are not dis-
similar to these children. From the fact that some of the
legends which sprang up around various saints are quite
certainly not genuine,[2] Fr Pierre Jounel and others conclude
that the saints in question never lived at all. They take no
notice of the fact that there are limits to historical research
in this area, and that, on the contrary, the appearance of the
legends shows that these are saints especially beloved by
ordinary people.

Isn't it the same in other cases? How many anec-
dotes and legends have sprung up around the figure of the
Prussian King Frederick II, not all of which are true. Did
he, therefore, perhaps never exist? No-one can doubt this,

---

1. First appeared under the title "Grenzen der historischen For-
schung" [The Limitations of Historical Research] in: *Anzeiger für
die katholische Geistlichkeit* no. 78 (1969) p. 302; J. Lengeling replied
opposing it, ibid. pp. 371-372; cf. my response, ibid. p. 496.

2. But these legends are sometimes most significant. What is
recounted in them is very often symbolic; cf. the legends of martyrs
at the end of my book *Zeugen des Herrn. Zeugnis der Märtyrer der
Frühkirche nach zeitgenössischen Gerichtsakten, Briefen und Berichten*
[Witnesses to the Lord. The Witness of Martyrs of the Early Church,
as found in Contemporary Accounts of their Trials, Letters and
Reports] (Waldstatt-Verlag, Einsiedeln/Switzerland), pp. 287-294.

since we have countless genuine sources both by him and about him. He only died less than two hundred years ago.

The further back we go in history, the more scanty the sources are in every area. Wars and disturbances have destroyed most archives, copies are often no longer extant. Thus it comes about that, for numerous early Christian martyrs and confessors, especially where the Roman ones are concerned, we either have no "acts" at all, or these survive only in extensively reworked versions.[3]

But is this sufficient ground on which to offer the saints in question less liturgical honour than formerly, despite the fact that their lives have been celebrated in the Mass, and by the Christian people, for centuries past? Saint George, for instance, or Saint Nicholas, to give just two examples. It is true that we know little about them for certain. The extent to which both were revered and honoured from the very beginning, however, is shown by the fact that the Eastern Church has chosen one as the model martyr, and the other as the model of a holy bishop. For centuries past their pictures have regularly decorated the iconostasis, and the Eastern and Western Churches have always been united in honouring them.

And now they want to allow only a local cult of either of them. Is their significance for the universal Church less, nowadays, than for instance the fashionable Italian saint Maria Goretti, who has now found entry into the calendar of saints? Nothing against this brave girl, but she certainly has not yet become a saint honoured throughout the Church, any more than the martyrs from the Far East, from Africa and from America.

If the availability, or on the other hand the lack, of genuine source material about a saint were to be decisive as far as a continuing cult were concerned, then to be consistent the feast of Saint Joachim and Saint Anne, or the

---

3. Concerning the Roman martyrs, compare the book just referred to, pp. 79-108. This gives the few surviving genuine acts of martyrs, classified according provinces, together with letters and other genuine witnesses.

feast of "the Sacrifice of Mary" (the Presentation of Mary in the Temple), would have to be removed from the calendar. Both feasts are based on legends, which are probably very old, but we can no longer establish whether they have a historically reliable basis. But what should decide the place of any given saint should be, in the first instance, the way he is revered amongst the people; unless, that is, we know for a fact that he never existed – which is not the case for any of the saints who have been "got rid of" – or it is demonstrable that he did not lead a holy life.

It is incomprehensible, what on earth anyone intends to achieve with the constant changes and innovations. Would it not have been sufficient, as the Benedictines have now been doing for decades, to declare the majority of saints' days to be "simple" feasts, and beyond this to permit the commemoration in the Mass of all those saints who are inscribed in the martyrology? In that way it would not have needed any great changes, and the door would have remained open for any further organic development. Doing it this way, however, something new is dictatorially imposed, even though people are still talking about overcoming the rubricism which has existed hitherto. In an age, in which attitudes exalting material comfort pose great dangers for the Church, in which besides this Professors of Theology who are tainted with unbelief are shaking the foundations of faith, we ought not to cause such additional disturbances amongst the faithful, as are now occasioned by the reshaping of the calendar of saints. Most believers do not see the point of these reforms, which are taking away from them just exactly those saints whom they had, up till now, revered the most.

Actuosa Participatio[1]

In the Constitution on the Sacred Liturgy of the Second Vatican Council is to be found an expression which has become the guiding principle for the current innovations in the domain of Liturgy, the "actuosa participatio," the active[2] participation of the faithful in the celebration of worship (no. 50). The call to do this is clearly expressed in I Peter 2:9; "But you are a chosen people, a royal priesthood, a holy race, a people claimed by God for his own, so that you may proclaim the mighty works of Him who called you out of darkness and into his marvellous light."

What the Council Fathers understood in detail by the term active participation, the same Constitution tells us a little earlier (no. 48):

> So the Church directs its entire attention to ensuring that Christians do not attend this mystery of the faith like outsiders who are merely looking on; they wish rather, to learn through the rites and the prayers of this mystery to understand rightly, and thus to join in celebrating the sacred action consciously, piously and actively, to let themselves be formed by the Word of God, and to have their strength renewed at the table of the Body of the Lord. They should give thanks to God not merely through the hands of the priest, but also in union with him, and should learn in this way to be able to offer themselves.

This exhortation was necessary, with regard to the practice in the Latin rite, especially in Romance-language countries. Here the faithful were, since the Middle Ages, merely mute onlookers at an official form of worship celebrated by the clergy (Mass, daily prayer) and could take an active part only in popular devotions, above all in praying the Rosary.

---

1. First appeared in: *Anzeiger für die Katholische Geistlichkeit* no.80 (1971) pp. 238-240.
2. [In English, the term "actual" is less misleading than "active," which is precisely the point Gamber makes in this chapter.]

Today however, especially with us in Germany, and yet more so in Holland and France, we have fallen into the other extreme, into an over-busy joining-in of the "People of God" in the Mass, and because of this, some elements which were hitherto essential in the performance of the sacred action, above all the choir, have been almost entirely excluded. Thus, in a strange fashion, the style of earlier non-liturgical worship, in which the priest prays aloud and the people make responses and sing hymns, has become a model for the way in which the active participation of the faithful at the Mass has been effected. This is the same form as was used in the thirties by Pius Parsch to construct his services of "People's Liturgy."

Matters are especially bad today, since the introduction of the new rite in the Romance-language countries. Here the people had hitherto hardly been used to taking any active part in worship. There are very few hymns. Since there were few instances where a reader or a choir were available, the celebrant had to take over their parts as well, in the new rite. Thus it comes about that the latter has to recite virtually the whole text of the Mass, that is to say the prayers, the readings and the hymns, and in most cases, in order for people to hear and understand him in the large churches, he has to speak all this into a microphone, which is placed on the lectern as well as on the altar. From a practical point of view, then, we have here nothing but a *Missa privata* which is spoken out loud and which dispenses with any kind of solemnity, since the faithful hardly even join in the responses. In Germany, it is often hardly much better in many country parishes.

At this point it is appropriate to say a little about the loudspeaker systems in churches. The ears of modern people are often "soaked" all day long with voices from one loudspeaker or another. The voices come forth from the radio, the television, loudspeakers in businesses, in shops, on railway stations and from publicity announcements. However practical it may be to have such a loudspeaker system in a church, its constant use contributes somehow to reducing people to "the masses." A direct form of address is in all circumstances more natural, and thus more effective in influencing people. Microphones should therefore only be used in churches when this seems to be absolutely necessary. The "missa cantata" which used to be performed, and the old-fashioned pulpits, made a loudspeaker system unnecessary in most cases.

The "performers" in worship are, as has already been mentioned above, not only the priest and the people, but also the reader, the choir (or schola) and if possible also a deacon. A quick look at the situation in the Eastern Church, where so much of what is original has been more faithfully maintained than in the West, will make this clear. Here, since the fourth century, it is in fact the deacon who urges the people to take an active part, by leading litanies and by the many calls to prayer which he utters.

But above all the choir has a special part to play within the Liturgy. Congregational singing, especially the singing of the usual hymns, will in the long term prove unsatisfying. Singing by the choir, on the other hand, not only contributes to the celebration the artistic element which is so important. It is this which makes a celebration "solemn;" but it also creates the pause requisite for the personal prayers of the faithful. This is not achieved simply by the silence at certain points of the Mass, which people are propagating nowadays. For the fact is that modern man frequently experiences silence merely as emptiness. He lacks the training for contemplative prayer. Solemn choral singing can however become for him a wave which will carry his personal prayer.

It is a mistake to suppose solemnity and active participation to be mutually exclusive. Anyone who attends a service of worship today comes into the church building from the common sense everyday world, and brings with him a need for solemnity. He is seeking an experience of the numinous. Yet at the same time, he wants to take an active part in the Liturgy, and not merely "to attend Mass prayerfully." Here it is a matter of finding a middle way between the passivity of an earlier time and what is often the over-active joining-in of today.

Solemnity is, of its nature, no enemy of natural behaviour. In the south you can experience the way that children come into church with balloons. Nobody takes offence at it. We ought not to ask too much of children in services of worship. We northerners are too unbending in God's House. We can learn at the festivals of Mediterranean countries how to hold a celebration in a community. There should be in the Liturgy something of the special feeling of a wedding, the special feeling of a natural celebration. Without this, active participation will become just a stiff fashion of ordering things. And, please, no false pathos, such as is easily introduced into a "spoken" celebration!

The Eastern Church never knew the period of gothic, with its overemphasis on private prayer as opposed to communal piety and religious practice, nor that of baroque, with its overdone ornamentation. On that account, there has never been a private Mass in the East, nor a service of worship without singing. And there, on the other hand, there are no orchestral Masses, as there are in the West. Certainly, it was a pity that in the East the "great mystery" came to the fore far too much, and that because of that, in some oriental rites the active participation of the people was almost entirely lost, in the course of time.

This was not, however, true of the area of Slavic culture, with its natural popular piety. Here the faithful, in village churches at least, joined in with the simple singing of the choir (in harmony) or of the cantor. Besides this, active participation was made easier here through the fact that the prayers, readings and songs were all in a language which, although it was a sacred language, was also to a great extent understood by the people.

As well as this, the individual who attends a service of worship in the Eastern Church has complete freedom to be present at the sacred action, which is carried out by the clergy in the first instance, after his own fashion. No-one will take offence if he comes into the church in the middle of the celebration, lights candles in front of the iconostasis, and throws himself down in humble prayer before the icons. On the other hand, he can stand silently behind one of the pillars, and experience the solemn Liturgy as a silent spectator. This kind of participation does not always necessarily mean that he is uninvolved, just as someone who goes to the theatre can follow the action on the stage, and shares in it by being inwardly moved.

Modern man, in particular, most urgently needs the freedom we have just described, which is now scarcely possible any longer, on account of current overemphasis on active participation in the Latin rite. This is quite often experienced, by those of the faithful who reflect and experience things more profoundly, simply as a preoccupation with externals, and as an over-busy joining-in, and thus rejected by them. They feel that they have been "handed over" to whatever is the style of worship and the manner of organising things of the current celebrant.

Hitherto, services of worship throughout the Church were celebrated according to fixed traditional rules, in following which a worthy celebration was ensured, providing at the same time some guarantee of a worship conducted in a liturgically unobjectionable manner. Now, the overemphasis on active participation has led in the West to a constant search for new ways of achieving an active sharing in the worship on the part of the faithful. Constant experimentation appears as a necessity, because the innovations which to start with make a certain impression on the faithful, are found in practice to lose their effect very quickly.

Permanence is of the essence of a liturgical rite.[3] No rite makes a spontaneous and immediate appearance, but gradually develops and then, like a good wine, it has finally "matured." Only in this way can it offer satisfaction to every participant, to the academic as well as the simple mother. Modern Liturgy, which often resembles the rationalistic Calvinist worship, most often gives expression to only one particular taste or style, which is that of the celebrant of that particular service. But a rite cannot, as we have just shown, simply be created. It develops slowly, over the course of centuries, and consequently takes account of all the factors at different times. But it must not be allowed

---

3. Cf. below the chapter "Continuity in Liturgical Development."

to stiffen into rubricism, in the way that happened in the West after the Council of Trent. A similar situation now obtains in some parts of the Eastern Church.

It would be interesting at some time to make a special study, investigating the question of adaptation of the rite in relation to what actually happens when it becomes stiffened in this way, and exactly why this happens. We must in any case ask ourselves, today, exactly why this or that feature developed in the way it has, especially with regard to the stronger emphasis on the cultic elements, or why certain forms of worship were done away with in the course of time. In some cases this happened at the same time, both in the Eastern and in the Western Church, as for example with discontinuing the practice of receiving Communion in the hand, which we will talk about in the next chapter.

On the other hand the danger remains of our learning nothing from history. There is also a danger that active participation does not bring as many benefits as perhaps it should do. In all attempts at something new, there is one thing we should not forget: a service of worship is primarily (Greek) "Leitourgia," that is to say, according to the usage of this word in the Septuagint, solemn service before God,[4] thus, a sacred event primarily relating to God. The faithful are to take their place in this event as "a holy people, a royal priesthood." But Liturgy could in itself equally be enacted without the faithful playing any part, since it is a matter of indifference how many people are engaged in carrying out the solemn service before God. The participants must be allowed the freedom to decide the extent to which they take part in the celebration. We should even tolerate the person praying silently in the corner. Someone like that may sometimes go "home rather more justified" (Luke 18:14) than other people who, from an external point of view, have taken an active part.

---

4. Cf. *Liturgisch Woordenboek II* [Liturgical Dictionary, vol. II] (Roermond, 1965/68), cols. 1573-74. In the Septuagint, "Leitourgia" never has the sense of "service (work done in the public service) of the people," which was its original meaning in Greek.

ACTUOSA PARTICIPATIO

The active participation of the faithful is, therefore, as we have tried to show, an essential element in the liturgical celebration. In order to enable it bring effective results, however, certain conditions are necessarily presupposed and must obtain. Amongst these are an appropriate allocation of rôles as between celebrant, deacon, reader, choir (schola) and faithful. It is also necessary to use a tested form of rite, which guarantees the kind of celebration which can be expected of any and every participant. This should produce a natural sense of celebration, and ought at the same time to guarantee for the individual attending a service of worship the greatest possible measure of freedom in relation to their degree of participation. But above all it should always be a service before God.

Active participation will certainly never be able to become a universal cure for all pastoral ailments. What is at least as important is solid instruction of the faithful in preaching and catechetical teaching. Nonetheless, if rightly understood, it can bring great pastoral benefits and, not least, it can contribute to the maturity of modern-day Christians.

Communion in the Hand
Yes or No?[1]

On the part of the official Church, a "leaflet" on this question has been published in Vienna, which is supposed to serve as a basis for instructing the faithful on this matter.[2] In this leaflet it is indicated that the change in practice for the receiving of Communion is not a matter of faith, not least because the practice of receiving Communion directly in the mouth first came into use "from the ninth century onwards."

This is correct. But if we want to be precise about it, we would have to say that a regional council at Rouen in the ninth century found it necessary to forbid the receiving of Communion in the hand by the laity, because this old custom of communicating in that way had lasted longer here than it had elsewhere. The practice of receiving Communion in the hand was in fact abandoned quite a long time earlier, to be exact from the fifth or sixth century onwards.

But we are by no means so much concerned here with this problem from the history of Liturgy. The question we posed above would in fact better have been formulated as follows: Is the introduction of Communion in the hand at the present time defensible from a pastoral point of view? We have made a point of saying: "at the present time." Any practice regarding the reception of Communion, which was at one time in general use in the Church as a whole, can never be rejected simply in itself.

The question we have now posed should be answered with a clear "No." Why is this? The "form of reception of Communion" is by no means, as it suggests in the "leaflet," "of secondary importance." The present-day demand for receiving Communion directly in the hand does in fact reveal a "turnaround in our attitude to the

---

1. First appeared in: *Anzeiger für die katholische Geistlichkeit*, no. 79 (1970) p. 326f.
2. The text is given in its entirety at the end of this chapter.

Eucharist." But this change in attitude, so it appears, consists in fact in the disappearance of faith in the Real Presence of Christ in the sacrament.

No doubt other ritual customs and habits, like for instance which colour of chasuble should be worn on a certain day, or the choice of readings for the Mass, are indeed of secondary importance. But never the manner in which we receive Communion. Especially when we reflect how strict the practice with respect to the veneration of the holy Eucharist has been hitherto. How great the care that was taken to keep even the smallest particle safe from being profaned, and how strict were the penalties for the desecration of the sacrament.

Thus, up until a few years ago laypeople were, officially, not even allowed to touch the consecrated chalice, even if it was empty. And today the Body of the Lord is placed in the hands, sometimes unwashed, of those same laypeople, a practice which means that one cannot always be sure what is now going to happen to the Sacred Host.

In this way we swing from one extreme to the other. Are the faithful not likely, in this fashion, to be troubled by doubts as to whether the Church does indeed still maintain the old concept? Where is the pastoral sense in this? This yawning gap between the two extremes is not something to be bridged with just a few words of instruction.

We live in an age which is characterised by a crisis of authority, in the secular sphere just as much as in the ecclesiastical. Associated with this is a frightening lack of reverence and respect, especially on the part of young people. And in addition to all this there is a crisis of faith, such as the Church has never before experienced to this extent, because it concerns the fundamental elements on which faith rests. Yet it is only in an age of great faith, that a change with such serious implications as that of the reintroduction of receiving Communion in the hand, can be made without endangering the piety of the faithful. That is to say, only when the faithful are entirely filled with reverence for this "mystery of the faith." And not in a time of crisis for the Church. The great majority of the bishops who were asked about this by the Pope recognised this quite

clearly, and therefore gave their vote against the reintroduction at the present time of receiving Communion in the
hand. Nevertheless, in certain countries people did not rest
until Apostolic See had signified its agreement.

In the "leaflet" we have been quoting, it says furthermore that the custom "of taking hold of the Host with
one's own hand, like an ordinary piece of bread," is "felt
by many people to be the simple and natural gesture which
best corresponds to this sign." A sign, a symbol, does not
demand the same reverence as would be appropriate for
the Body of the Lord. But is the Holy Eucharist now merely
a sign? In that case, those responsible for the leaflet would
be right.

It would be of some importance to investigate why,
both in the East and in the West, the old practice of receiving Communion was discontinued. The change from leav-
ened to unleavened bread can not have been the real reason
for it, as J.A. Jungmann suggests in his book *Missarum Sollemnia*, since the change to unleavened bread was never
effected in the Eastern Church. An exaggerated emphasis
on the "holiness of the Eucharistic Gift," which is mentioned in the "leaflet" as a possible reason, equally cannot
have provided the impulse, since this holiness has never
been called into question. Furthermore, at least for the early
Middle Ages, that is, the time when the change was made
in the manner of giving Communion, the reproach that
"the idea that this is given us to feed upon, as Bread for
the Life of the world" faded into the background, is equally
inapplicable.

We are more likely to find that the real reason is
that people's experience of lay people receiving Communion in their hand had not been at all encouraging. Since
the fifth century, above all, when congregations grew very
quickly, and then even more so later, when practically all
the inhabitants of a place, good and bad, were members of
the Church.

The experiences they had will be the same as are
happening today, and will increasingly occur: from a lack
of reverence at the reception right up to the misuse of the
Holy Eucharist for superstitious, even satanic ends (satanic

masses!). One occurrence still sounds harmless, which happened only recently: an eight-year-old girl took the Host
back home with her, so that her favourite playfellow, a little
dog, could also have Communion.

After the Church as a whole abandoned the practice
of receiving Communion in the hand in the early Middle
Ages, we cannot reverse such a step today without having
serious reasons for doing so. Certainly not, when we take
the Eastern Church into account, which has no thought of
changing its practice regarding Communion. The reasons
we have at the moment for continuing to give Communion directly in the mouth are far more important than those
which can be advanced for the reintroduction of Communion in the hand.

Are there truly no more pressing problems in the
Church today, than making a change in the way that Communion is given out? But it seems as if people are avoiding
the more difficult reforms. Instead of this we are experiencing a series of "mini-reforms" as if they are coming off
a production line. Real reforms would be able to help the
Church in the present crisis, but apparent reforms will only
damage her to the same extent.

We live today in a time of constant change. This may
be entirely useful in some areas, as for instance in technology and medicine, but in other areas it clearly shows itself
to be damaging. One thing is certain: unceasing changes
in the form of worship arouse in the faithful a feeling of
insecurity, an insecurity which spreads out from the area of
worship all across the foundations of the faith, since most
people are unable to distinguish what is essential from
what is inessential.

Today, the enemies of the church are attempting to
accomplish their work of destruction no longer, as hitherto,
from without, but from within. They want to "change the
Church's function." The procedure of permanent change
helps them with this, because with this nothing is kept in
the form people are used to, not even small and insignifi-
cant things. In this way, Christians who have been made to
feel uncertain fall an easy prey to unbelief.

In the past few centuries, the Catholic Church has

stood like a rock against the surging waves of unbelief and error. Perhaps she was sometimes too hard. But woe to her, if she turns into a sponge, which greedily sucks up every innovation – however promising they may appear at first glance. And certainly we have to do with just such an untimely innovation in the case of the reintroduction of Communion in the hand. Yet perhaps the early Christian practice will come to have a positive significance for the "little flock" which, after all this, will be all that is left of the Western Church in the future.

Appendix

*Leaflet announcing that receiving Communion in the hand
will now also be permissible.*

The manner in which Holy Communion should be administered and received was neither laid down by Christ, nor has it been determined by a decision of the Church's Magisterium. She has never regarded this as a question of faith, but rather a question of the right ordering of the Liturgy, and, as such, as being subject in any case to alteration.

In comparison with the problems which confront the Church today, along with the whole of mankind, no doubt the question as to the kind of way in which Communion is received will seem of lesser importance. It would nevertheless be wrong to suppose that it merely originates in the urge for innovation which is so widespread nowadays. The custom of receiving Communion in the hand has not been invented in our own time. For centuries it was the general practice to give out Communion into people's hands. Even the institution of the Holy Eucharist by Christ, at the Last Supper, proceeded in accordance with the table manners which were customary at that period and in that country.

The custom of presenting Communion to the mouth began to spread from the ninth century onwards. The reasons for this were many and various. But at Holy Communion, both the person distributing Communion and the person receiving it must do so with all the care and reverence appropriate for the Body of Christ, and this is the case in every age, and whatever the manner of administration.

The most important reason for the transition from administration of Communion in the hand, to directly in the mouth, was the change in people's attitude to the Eucharist: The sense of the holiness of the eucharistic gift came to the fore; whilst the thought that this is given to nourish us, as "bread for the life of the world," faded into the background. This was connected with the reduction in the frequency of Communion; it was no longer seen as being self-evident that the congregation at the Sacrifice of the Mass also shared in the sacrificial meal. This resulted not merely from a tepid or indifferent attitude, but also from a feeling of unworthiness, even when the individuals were not aware of any grave fault in themselves. Thus the idea could easily take root, that reception of Communion directly in the mouth was more appropriate than receiving it in the hand.

When, therefore, in the years following the Council, a desire was felt for the reintroduction of Communion in the hand, that is similarly an indication that a change in eucharistic piety is once more coming about. Therefore it is that the receiving of the Host directly in one's own hand, just like ordinary bread, is felt by many people to be the simple and natural gesture which best corresponds to this sign. But the acclamation in use today after the consecration – "the Mystery of Faith" – is equally true here. The more simple our outward action, the greater and more urgent the demand made on our faith, which now expresses itself in the "Amen" with which we reply to what the priest says in presenting it to us: "The Body of Christ." It is in any case true that each of the faithful has the right to receive Communion in the manner which best corresponds to his own particular religious sensitivity, that is to say, whether kneeling or standing, directly in the mouth or in the hand. And each will be able to say: I do this, just as the whole of Christendom has done it for centuries before me.

The Office of the Archbishop (Vienna) April 1970

Another word concerning the introduction
of Communion in the hand[3]

I entirely agree with everything that Dr. Klaus Gamber, of Regensburg, wrote in the August issue concerning Communion in the hand. Nonetheless I would like to suggest two further aspects for your consideration and reflection:

1. How does it come that there is a two-thirds majority of the German bishops in favour of giving permission for the receiving of Communion in the hand, contrary to the majority of bishops in the world as a whole? In his detailed discussion of 1970, "So-called Communion in the Hand," Professor Mey has established that the Instruction "Memoriale Domini," signed by the Pope on the 28th May 1969, of which the full text has been published hardly anywhere, obviously represents a revised version. The first part of the Instruction is quite unequivocal, and rejects the introduction of Communion in the hand, on the basis of the vote of the bishops of the world. Between the 19th March, when the response to the questionnaire sent to all the Latin bishops of the world was collated, and the 28th May – thus Professor Mey surmises, and not without reason – the advocates of Communion in the hand must have taken the Vatican by storm with the argument that, in their dioceses, the practice of receiving Communion in the hand had taken root so firmly that this development could no longer be reversed. That must then have led, he says, to the addition of the supplement, "sicubi vero contrarius usus, sanctam nempe Communionem in manibus ponendi, iam invaluerit" (that is, "wherever any usage to the contrary, that is to say, the receiving of Holy Communion in the hand, has already become fully accepted"), so as to give way to this demand, but with the restriction, which is otherwise unusual, that it should not be the Conference of Bishops which proposes this change which is to make the final decision, but each bishop for his own diocese.

---

3. Reader's letter in response to my article, published in: *Anzeiger für die katholische Geistlichkeit* no. 79 (1970) pp. 418-420.

COMMUNION IN THE HAND - YES OR NO?

Does this mean the introduction of Communion in the hand in the whole of Germany in general? No! Experience teaches us, of course, that it is impossible for one bishop to forbid Communion in the hand (in the way the Church as a whole does), if his neighbour allows it. The whole business is already quite difficult in other German-speaking areas (Austria, Switzerland) where Communion in the hand is not permitted. The Archbishop of Salzburg has already found it necessary to make it clear, on two occasions, by means of the official diocesan notice-sheet, and by notices put up on church doors, that the existing custom of giving Communion directly into the mouth of the communicant is being retained, and that even guests from other countries will have to conform to "this single unified practice." He is likely to have little success with this, if there are further cases of notorious disobedience being accorded the dignity of legislation which subsequently legalises it. But we will look at that later.

At this point we would like to float the question, of what really was the position with the "usage to the contrary," that is to say, receiving Communion in the hand, having "already become fully accepted" in Germany. Nothing is known of any sounding of opinion amongst the laity, nor even merely among the clergy. This is where, if anywhere, the "democracy" which is so often referred to would have been appropriate. Millions of Deutschmarks are spent on conducting an extremely questionable "survey" amongst the faithful, in relation to the synod which is soon to be held, a survey which for many of the faithful is far too demanding...

But in the question of choosing between Communion in the hand or directly in the mouth, every one of the faithful who is actually a communicant would have been capable of making a genuine personal choice. Why was such a survey of opinion not undertaken? There is only one answer: because the advocates of Communion in the hand knew beforehand, with some certainty, that the response would have been negative. No-one will dare to assert that in any one of the larger churches in Germany the receiving of Communion in the hand was, before the granting of permission, already so firmly established and customary that there would have been no way or repressing it. Where it was practised, then at most these were little private groups, and even then at the insistence of progressivist clergy, not in the first instance of the laity. There is no way, then, that we can talk about this being generally practised. Yet according to the clear and explicit wording of the Instruction, this is the basis for the papal indult, which was in any case insisted upon in the face of fierce opposition from the Prefect of the Congregation of Rites, Cardinal Gut. If the latter had, as is the custom nowadays, appealed to his conscience in "constructive disobedience," then he would not have signed the decree...

2. But this is the most questionable aspect of the affair, that is to say, that a usage is introduced, by means of the salami-technique, by way of an abuse. The call both to Rome and to the bishops is becoming ever louder, from amongst both priestly and lay circles, to call a halt, and no longer to tolerate in practice any "anticipatory disobedience" (that is: the most barefaced disobedience, which is now being openly encouraged by Professors of Theology), to tolerate none whatever. It is of course a distasteful matter, and a difficult question of conscience for each individual bishop, as to whether he should suspend his priests for disobedience in liturgical matters after repeated warnings. But if things continue the way they are, then he will in the long term be unable to evade the question, and the longer one delays, then the more difficult it becomes – there will be total confusion in the Church. It is not the reform of the Liturgy as such, nor even the new *Ordo Missæ*, if it had been introduced correctly (including the Latin Mass and the Roman Canon) and *uniformly* in the whole of the Latin Church, that has brought about the disunity which can be seen today at every Communion rail (unless the Priest has compelled his congregation to receive Communion in the hand, against the clear wording of the Instruction), but the wilfulness which amounts to disobedience...

Any authority which silently tolerates disobedience is surrendering its own position.

Monsignor Professor Rudolf Peil, Odenthal

Making Worship Relevant?[1]

In a parish in northern Germany, a little while ago, a curate who was celebrating a Youth Mass replaced the liturgical Creed with a profession of faith by the pop singer Udo Jürgens. We come across other instances of this, less crass perhaps but nonetheless shocking, all the time now. This is why we feel we must ask a fundamental question: Is it necessary to make the Liturgy relevant nowadays, and is this to be recommended?

Modern people are obsessed by the idea that everything must reflect the so-called "modern day," the new attitude to life: architecture and literature, art and music. But just as people nowadays race about the world in fast cars, without, so far as the majority are concerned, truly experiencing it and marvelling at it, so, very often, what is presented as the expression of modern attitudes to life is superficial and empty.

Along with this there is the hectic and unceasing hunt for novelty and sensation. Only what is contemporary matters. And what is contemporary has mostly been forgotten by tomorrow. Never the same thing twice! Being "up to date," that is the slogan.

It is ever more loudly asserted that the Liturgy, too, should be infused with the Spirit of the Age and should speak the same language as modern man. No longer, we are told, should it be a "liturgical museum piece."

---

1. First appeared in: *Anzeiger für die katholische Geistlichkeit* no. 79 (1970) pp. 91-92.
[Translator's Note: One meaning of "aktualisieren" is "to make something immediate" or "to make relevant;" another meaning is "to update," "to bring up to date." Thus, "Aktualisierung" (the German word used in the title here) is the normal German translation of Pope John XXIII's "Aggiornamento;" this would be in the minds of German Catholic readers.

People base their claim on the fact that the Roman rite, when it was first developed, was equally a product of its own time, that it made use of forms which then, in the period of Late Antiquity, were customary. People say that it is sheer historical sentimentality if we go on using the old rituals, the old texts and melodies, and are reluctant to make worship contemporary and relevant.

It is true that the Roman rite, as it existed hitherto – though doubtless a masterpiece – reflects the style and sensibilities of late Antiquity and of the early Middle Ages. It is a pity that its forms became to a great extent set and fixed so early on.

In contrast to this, the Byzantine Liturgy, and most of the oriental rites, reached their final form considerably later than did the Roman rite. The creative impulse was not quenched in the Eastern Church until the beginning of the modern age. That is how it comes about that they have hardly any problem with the Liturgy, in the way we have. One difficulty is simply the length of many services, together with the question as to which parts might, if necessary, be shortened.

The claim that in future the Roman rite should no longer be the only rite in use in the Church as a whole is certainly also justified. And when it was being shaped, it was certainly never intended for that. It was only later that it became the uniform rite for Western Europe and the New World, and that of the Church in missionary countries. There is no doubt that this was an unfortunate development, although we cannot overlook the universal dimension to this, particularly today, when, with improved communications, people and nations are drawing ever closer to each other.

In this respect, too, things are more favourable in the Oriental Churches. Here there is no uniform rite, but a variety of liturgical forms, allowing virtually every people to develop their own rite, suitable for their national character.

It never occurred to Pope Gregory the Great (†604) – to whose reform of the Liturgy, as is well known, most of the texts and rites in use in the Roman Church until very recently date back – that his liturgical books and liturgical reforms would ever be in force beyond the boundaries of the archdiocese of Rome. Quite the contrary. His saying is well known (Epistle 1:13) "In una fide nil officit ecclesiæ consuetudo diversa." In English, roughly: "If unity of belief is preserved, then a diversity of (ritual) customs does no harm to the Church."

If, today, the demand is made in various ways that the Liturgy should be more firmly rooted in the congregation, that it should be possible – to put it in concrete terms – to give spontaneous formulation to prayers and intercessions, then we can refer to the fact that these practices were not unknown to the Roman Liturgy in its beginnings, although not by any means to the same extent as is sometimes demanded nowadays.

This is quite clearly evidenced by the prayers in the Leonianum, a collection of prayers for the Mass written by the popes of the period before Gregory the Great. But these texts were not spontaneously formulated prayers, they were, rather, written in advance of the celebration by the clergyman presiding, and the latter quite often pays some attention to the problems of the day.[2]

Above and beyond this, it is probable that in the early Church not only the president, but also individual members of the congregation prayed aloud, both spontaneous confessions of faith in Christ, and thanksgivings, in the course of the Holy Supper, thanks to the charismatic gifts bestowed upon them by the Holy Spirit (cf. I Corinthians 14). The disappearance from within the Church of charismatic gifts like these is one of the reasons for liturgical texts becoming fixed, as the Liturgy developed – this happened for the most part from the fourth century onwards – until, in the end, hardly anything new was written any more.[3]

This does mean, on the other hand, that the spontaneous formulation of prayers in the course of the Liturgy, whether by the presiding minister or by a member of the

---

2. Cf. A. Stuiber, *Libelli Sacramentorum Romani* (Bonn, 1950).
3. Cf. K. Gamber, *Codices liturgici latini antiquiores* (Freiburg, Switzerland, 1968) especially p. 25ff.

congregation, does assume a special gift. This, again, is the fruit of a faith which goes beyond what we commonly find by way of faith amongst Christians. There is otherwise a great danger that these spontaneously formulated prayers, however relevant, will take as their starting-point all the events and the cogitations that we read about in the newspapers, and not the belief in the Triune God, the hope of the resurrection, and the expectation of the Kingdom of Christ.

Those who advocate steps to make the Liturgy relevant too easily forget that the Western world is no longer undivided. But you don't help a sick man by making him even weaker and more unsure than he already is in himself. However that is exactly what people are doing today. They are removing more and more of what was previously regarded as the basic foundations, and are trying to save a Church whose faith is weak with new and untried liturgical forms.

For all that, new liturgical forms ought not to be simply rejected on principle. A competent doctor will not remain content with the old-fashioned methods for dealing with illnesses. He will, rather, act in accordance with the current state of medical research, and will use for his patients whatever new treatments this has to offer – assuming, of course, that they have been properly tested.

The current-day innovators in forms of worship, who mostly belong to the younger generation, do not take such a responsible approach. Usually without convincing reasons, from pure desire for innovation and taking pleasure in experimentation, they abandon the well-tried old forms – even in the teeth of resistance from the members of their own congregation in the pews – and replace them, quite obviously bereft of any psychological understanding whatever, with material that is untried, or even quite questionable.

Is it likely to bring a blessing for the Church, making the Liturgy "relevant" in such a way? One certainly cannot deny the good intentions of many of the modern enthusiasts, but the results of their iconoclasm turn out to be more and more destructive, and destructive not only of the forms of worship in use hitherto, but of the Church itself. Faith and Liturgy exercise a reciprocal influence on each other. A well-founded faith is the only basis for an effective Liturgy, just as, contrariwise, no Liturgy, be it never so solemn and so lovely, can rescue anyone's faith.

But does the Liturgy need to be the expression of its period at all? This question is interconnected with another, the question as to the essence of the Liturgy. To put it plainly: is the Liturgy primarily a service provided for people, or service to God, that is, worship? The cultic element is nowadays deliberately overlooked, and the Liturgy is regarded as above all a service provided for people: in proclamation of the Word and celebration of the Supper.

If Liturgy really were primarily a service provided for people, then it would be logical for it to be constantly updated and made relevant. Providing a service for people is not, however, the first task of the Liturgy. It is the task of the preaching activity of the Church as such: in sermons, in teaching in schools, in religious lectures and discussions, nowadays above all in the press, and on the radio and television.

The Liturgy is only one part, and indeed a small part, of the proclamation of the Gospel which Christ commanded the Church to carry out. It is, as we have already emphasised, primarily the service of God. The Mass is more than that: it is a sacramental celebration, it imparts a sharing in the divine life, it is – not least – the Church's sacrifice.

The cult directed to God has nonetheless some significance for man, and in particular for modern man. This cult should, by its sublime solemnity, lift man out of the everyday, common-sense world, should take hold of him in his inner being and bring him close to God. Current-day man, harassed by deadlines and appointments and by the chase after money, needs an oasis of peace and quiet, in opposition to the restlessness of the world.

Thus, many people who come to church prefer apparent inactivity to the all too active busyness of many "modern" services. This latter is often more of a hindrance than a help.

It is certainly foolish to think that, by goading the participants into activity and by constantly dragging into worship the forms current in the world, one can make these services more attractive, especially amongst younger people, in the way that people are attempting in many places, especially by rock-Masses. An experiment like that will attract young people a couple of times out of sheer curiosity, then after that they will stay away. Young people who like rock music don't look for it in church, but in pubs and clubs. The fact is that it is much "better" there. In the long term, young people come to church only on account of religious beliefs.

But we should not on that account entirely exclude any attempt to modify the forms of worship. This has happened successfully many times in the past, or at least it was not hindered, even in the period of rubricism. We only have to think of the influence of baroque on the way Mass was celebrated, for instance in the orchestral Masses, which conformed to contemporary tastes.

But the Liturgy, as a cultic celebration, must at the same time stand above any period and the cultural tastes of the period. For as such a celebration it is subject to rules quite different from those governing a preaching of the faith. Whilst the latter has no need to be subject to any "ceremonial" rules whatever, and should be as "relevant" as possible, the Liturgy, as a cultic celebration, is associated with certain forms which have been handed-down.

Each and every cultic celebration is therefore antiquated to a certain extent – it would be better to say: it is timeless. Indeed it has to be, since it is no everyday activity which is consummated therein, but an act which stands beyond time, since it is directed toward God.

The forms of worship, of the cult, as a whole, are certainly not unchangeable. But at no point in the history of Christian worship has there been a definite break in development. At least, not up till now. It is much more a matter of organic development.

Now, however, all that has gone before is being questioned by a group of liturgists. The traditional rituals are being subjected to rational examination, one after the other. Some, above all the historians, want to restore them; others, the practical pastors, want to make them suitable for the present day. Anything which fails to stand up to the critical examination of the reformers is being changed, or even jettisoned, especially of course whatever no longer seems to be contemporary, and therefore no longer "relevant."

In place of the organic development which has taken place hitherto, there is now constant experimentation. And every liturgist thinks he has to be creatively involved – "in anticipatory obedience," as they say – in all this, in the same way as that curate whom we talked about at the start of our discussion.

Do not be surprised, then, if in a very short time we find ourselves standing before an enormous heap of rubble – not only in the sphere of the Liturgy!

Continuity in Liturgical Development[1]

Is it possible to create an entirely new Liturgy? In view of the constant innovations in the sphere of worship, one would have to put that basic question with all possible emphasis. One is inclined to refer to what we are now experiencing, quite directly, as the "manufacture of Liturgy." "Manufacture" is connected with "factory," with "teamwork" and production line. This is the teamwork of a relatively small group of liturgists, who for some years now have provided us with new forms off their production-line. How different the process of development was in past centuries!

In their origins, the forms of Christian worship, so far as their relation to Judaism was concerned, were nothing fundamentally new. Just as, in the areas of dogma and of law, the Primitive Church only gradually freed itself from the synagogue, so similarly the liturgical forms freed themselves from the Jewish rites. This is equally true of the eucharistic celebration, which has an evident relationship to the ritual meals of the Jews, and of the oldest parts of the daily prayer, which builds on the daily prayer of the synagogue.

The belief in the Risen Jesus led to the break with the synagogue. In ritual questions, on the other hand, there were at first hardly any points of dispute with the Jews. Thus, the Apostles, together with the newly baptised members, continued to take part in the worship in the Temple after the feast of Pentecost (cf. Acts 2:46). Thus, likewise, Paul, together with four men, took on the Nazirite's vows and had the prescribed offering made (Acts 21:23-26).

What was really new in Christian worship, the commemoration of the Lord in the re-enactment of what was done at the Last Supper, became organically connected with the Jewish ritual of breaking of bread, which happened all the more easily since Jesus himself, at the supper on the

1. First appeared in: *Anzeiger für die katholische Geistlichkeit* no. 78 (1969) pp. 372-373.

evening before his Passion, kept to the ritual of the festival meals of the Jews.

What has been said about the Primitive Church is correspondingly true of the Early Church. Certainly, the same liturgical texts were not used everywhere in the first three centuries – a great deal of freedom was left to the celebrant in this, and also to the particular congregation. In the ritual itself, however, pretty well no changes were made at that time. What problems arose within the Church when, for instance, in the second century the date of Easter was changed, and the Pasch was no longer celebrated on the same day as that of the Jews! It almost came to a permanent schism with the conservative Churches of Asia Minor, at that time.

Not until, in the period after the time of Constantine, as a result of mass conversions, the number of believers grew rapidly and they were no longer able to come together in a small group, as they had been accustomed to do, did changes in the rite become necessary. The meetings for worship now had to be transferred from the houses where they had previously been held into newly-built churches. But it does seem as though this was accomplished without any great alterations. At any rate, in contrast to the dispute about the date of Easter, we hear nothing of any disputes concerning ritual in the Church at that period.

After Christianity had become the state religion, this resulted in a much fuller elaboration of the cult. The art of choral singing began to flourish in church, and the use of incense was introduced. This greater elaboration led besides to the development of various separate rites, especially in the East, which in their essentials have survived in this form from late Antiquity down to the present day. But this development seems to have taken place, by and large, in organic fashion, at any rate without any interference or intervention to direct the course of things on the part of the ecclesiastical authorities. In their regional councils the authorities were concerned first and foremost to dispose of any possible abuses in worship.

Things did not change until the age of "rubricism," as the period of liturgical history after the Council of Trent has been called. There was no longer any organic development in the particular local Churches. At the order of pope Pius V (1566-72) a Mass-book for uniform use, the *Missale Romanum*, was created, which came into use quite quickly over almost the whole of the West. Each and every change to the prayers and rubrics now had to receive the express approval of the Congregation of Rites. It is worth emphasising in this connection that in the Curia they were always concerned to protect and promote the old Roman rite.

The Western Church, which could in addition mark up great successes in the various missionary fields, was bound in the end to find this traditional rite too tight a corset. At the Second Vatican Council ways forward were therefore sought which might lead towards new liturgical forms suited to the changed circumstances. No objection could be made to this in itself. In the course of applying in practice the decisions made at the Council, however, the previous organic development of the forms of worship has been to a great extent abandoned, and we have launched out into the sphere of large-scale experimentation.

In doing this, we were joining in a "trend" which is observable nowadays in all areas of life, in art no less than in technology and medicine. Everywhere the old forms and old methods are being abandoned in a search for new ones. But we should not overlook the fact that Liturgy is subject to quite different laws from technology or medicine, for instance, where experiments lead to progress.

Just as nowadays people tear down old and valuable buildings, in order to replace them with modern constructions which say nothing to us, although the old ones could just as easily have been restored, so it is happening with the Liturgy. People are simply getting rid of what they see as old-fashioned, and making new things as fast as a production-line. The only standard of judgement is the personal opinion of a group of "Liturgy manufacturers," who create new forms on the basis of their own, often narrow, view of things. One has the impression that they don't take the trouble to study the history of worship in any detail, so as to discover why the previous forms of the cult developed as they did.

Thus, liturgical forms are being reintroduced today, which in the course of previous development have shown that in the long term they cannot be tolerated, such as for instance giving the cup to the laity when there is a large number of communicants. We also need to investigate just why, in the Eastern and the Western Church, the early Christian custom of giving Holy Communion to lay people in their open hand was abandoned.

The manufacture of new liturgical formularies has shown itself to be no less problematical, when insufficient distinction is made between the text for a Church celebration that takes place just once, such as an ecumenical service of worship, and the official, oft-repeated rites of the Church.

A striking example is the "Liturgy for Holy Week," which has recently been published in provisional form and is already in use in many dioceses. Let us recall: It is not even fifteen years since, on the 16th November 1955, the decree on the renewal of Holy Week appeared. At that time changes in the rites and in the prayers were made, which were in part good and justifiable, like the time for the Easter Vigil to be held, but in part originated merely in the whim of those "Liturgy producers" of the time, like the way that the consecration of the Paschal Candle was elaborated, or the office of Easter Lauds at the close of the celebration.

At the same time, by this decree, the old rite of the *Hebdomada Sancta* has been done away with. Thus a form of the celebration of Holy Week which has been practised unchanged in the West for centuries, and was well-established here, has come to an end. It would have been a much happier idea to leave the rite as it had been up to now, and to wait for further developments. It could have been adapted meanwhile to the changed circumstances, by allowing a great deal "ad libitum," for instance by permitting the previous series of twelve prophetic readings to be reduced, or by the partial use of the vernacular.

It is quite clear, from the introductory rubric, how far the new rite of Easter, as against that of the year 1955, reflects the personal tastes of those who have created it, when it says:

> On Holy Saturday the Church keeps vigil at the tomb of the Lord, and contemplates his suffering and death. The altar remains uncovered, and there is no celebration of the eucharistic sacrifice. Not until after the Vigil, when in the night-time we await the Resurrection, comes the expression of Easter joy, which may then be unfolded in all its fullness in the course of fifty days.

The source for this strange rubric is quite clearly "The Year of Grace" by Pius Parsch. What in his case was merely an interpretation has now become a guideline, a rubric. But did the Early Church really wait for the Resurrection of the Lord, which is after all a historical fact, in the night of Easter? On that night they awaited only the return of Christ. But in the new celebration of Easter (apart from in rubric number 95) there is almost nothing of this basic idea to be found.

And we find here little of the radiant joy over the Resurrection of the Lord, the consciousness of victory, which we meet, we would almost be inclined to say, in an inimitable way, in the Liturgy for Easter Night of the Eastern Church. Here, the hymnic element is predominant, with that hymn ever again breaking through, which the priest has intoned at the door of the church, at the opening of the celebration: "Christ has risen from the dead. Through his death he has overcome death, and has given life to those in the grave." And in this celebration there is no lack of elements of what one would call particularly folk-traditional character, like the procession around the church, past the graves of the dead.

The celebration of Baptism takes a particularly prominent place in this very new rite. In the fourth and fifth centuries, when there were large numbers of adult candidates for Baptism, the connection of Baptism with the Resurrection was comprehensible. It may be appropriate nowadays for missionary countries as well. In our case, however, when at most there are a couple of children brought to be baptised on Easter Night, and there are mostly no adult candidates at all, this is a matter of artificially resurrecting an Early Christian custom.

It seems in any case to be certain: the new celebration of Easter Night will no more become a folk tradition, than that of 1955 or the old Holy Saturday Liturgy. Here in Germany there used to be a celebration of the Resurrection, therefore, on the evening before Easter, or early in the morning. We do not want to talk about reintroducing this non-liturgical service. But you cannot deny that the celebration of the Resurrection with the decorations and the visit to the holy tomb was a folk tradition, and had a great deal in common with the Easter Night Liturgy of the Eastern Church, to which we have referred, which is likewise much beloved of the people and is the best-attended service of the whole year, just as with us the Midnight Mass is.

Fifteen years ago, as we said, they "fabricated" a new Liturgy of Holy Week. It has obviously not stood the test, as is shown by the fact that already, after such a short space of time, they are designing a new one. These forms, too, will not last long. You cannot simply create a new rite from the foundations up. A ritual arises, it develops, it grows organically from already existing forms, and it atrophies when its time is past.

What has been said with regard to the Easter Night celebration, is equally applicable to the new missal and breviary. Would it not have been sufficient to allow some parts to be "ad libitum" here, instead of autocratically introducing new and untested material? As far as anyone can see, these new liturgical books will quickly show themselves to be of no practical use, because in the meantime they are bound to have had some new idea about how they should be written. Let us hope that those suggestions, after a more thorough study of the history of Liturgy, will be better than the ones made so far!

The Ecumenical Liturgy
of the Day After Tomorrow[1]

In the course of the conversations during the Council a new concept made its appearance: Ecumenical Liturgy.[2] We are becoming ever more aware that a simple re-ordering of the rubrics, possibly reintroducing parts of old formulae, and a merely makeshift adaptation of the rites to the circumstances of the times, so far as they can be foreseen, are no longer sufficient to resolve the serious difficulties which arise with respect to the Liturgy from the world-wide mission and constitution of the Church in modern times. The quite justified concerns of the bishops in the developing countries, and, by no means least, the knowledge of the liturgical wealth of the Eastern Churches, and the significance which they thus necessarily have, on that account, for the Church as a whole, burst apart the narrow frame of western spirituality, as became clear again and again in the Council's debates.

In the foreseeable future it will not suffice, merely to stick new patches on old clothes, and at some points to have recourse to earlier traditions. The Liturgy of the day after tomorrow must be an ecumenical Liturgy. What does that mean to say? The new Liturgy must bring to the Church, amongst all the many peoples of the earth, that unity of rite which we had hitherto glimpsed as being already established in the Roman Liturgy, with its

---

1. First appeared in the supplement "Christ in the World" to the Regensburg *Tages-Anzeiger* [Daily Gazette] of the 3rd/4th October, 1964. I developed these ideas further in my book, which has several times been referred to, *Liturgie übermorgen* [Liturgy the Day after Tomorrow] (1966).

2. [Translator's note: we need to understand that the term "ecumenical" is here being used in the same sense as in the title of Vatican II, as an "Ecumenical Council:" that is, "comprehending, or relating to, the whole of the world-wide Church in Communion with the Bishop of Rome." It has no direct connection with the idea of an "inter-Church" Liturgy which might, for instance, conceivably be suitable for use by Greek Orthodox as well as by Roman Catholics.]

liturgical language of Latin, which was celebrated almost everywhere in the world. We need not explain here in detail the reasons why, from a world-wide perspective, the Roman Liturgy in its previous form is no longer adequate to meet the demands of the modern age. The correctness of that view of the situation which we have mentioned is impressively demonstrated by the hard struggle the Council Fathers had with the schema on the Liturgy.

What should the ecumenical Liturgy look like? In quite general terms, it must be so simple in its construction, and in its forms and symbols must speak so clearly, that it can be understood by all peoples, and they can fully share in celebrating it. It must not be so artificial and complicated, that only with a great "liturgical apparatus" of clergy and singers is it possible to perform it in its full version. The ecumenical Liturgy must be a true people's Liturgy. Yet at the same time it must have such a style, and such a devotional element, that it lifts people out of their common sense everyday life, and "exalts" them in the true sense of the word.

As far as concerns the details of the ecumenical Liturgy, the question immediately arises, whether we should, as is happening nowadays in many areas of Church life and of public life, strike out in entirely new paths, and seek new forms, or whether we should start from ritual customs in current use, or, as the case may be, have recourse to older traditions. Even if the new form of worship is supposed to be in some sense "modern," and must in some sense be modern, nonetheless we should feel that an entirely new construction can be excluded. Since, for many and various reasons, the present Roman rite cannot offer any suitable basis for a genuinely ecumenical Liturgy, there remains the option of looking back to the earliest rite. But we should not fall into the error of historical sentiment. Not all old rites are appropriate for the modern age, nor suitable for putting into practice, any more than all later usages need to be set aside simply because they are more recent. Both the scholar and the practitioner need to co-operate in working out what the ecumenical rite should be like, if it is to be a real "masterpiece." All the efforts directed towards achieving a new form of worship will have to be informed both by the insights of the latest liturgical research, and by a respect for certain basic principles in liturgical celebration.

The simple form of worship used in the Early Church, as it was celebrated right up to the end of the era of persecution, should certainly be set aside from consideration. It was meant in the first instance for a small circle of believers with idealistic attitudes, and for assemblies in private houses. Equally, the forms of worship which took shape during the Middle Ages, with its piety coloured by subjectivity, are certainly not suitable to provide a basis for an ecumenical Liturgy. In the same way, there can scarcely be any question of taking over the Eastern Rites, despite their beauty, since they, just like the Western forms of worship we have just referred to, are a part of the spiritual attitude of a certain epoch. At the same time, we ought not to exclude the possibility that we might sometimes turn to this or that custom of the Eastern Church.

The "classical" Liturgy of the fourth and fifth centuries, however, could offer a starting-point for the creation of an ecumenical Liturgy. At that time it was already ecumenical, that is, as far as its structure is concerned it was celebrated in all parts of the Church in almost exactly the same way. In the phrasing of particular prayers there was on the contrary an extensive diversity of expression. Just as in the Primitive Church, at that time it was still left up to the celebrant (the bishop) to formulate many of the prayers as he chose, even though in some Churches here and there they already used Mass-books with their own forms of prayer, yet without these having being introduced for official use.

There is another reason why the classical Liturgy might serve as a model for the ecumenical Liturgy, and that is on account of its simple construction, which anyone can see and grasp. The ecumenical Liturgy should be, and is intended to be, no more than a framework of Liturgy, that is, it merely sets up the basic forms which are to be respected in the universal Church throughout the world. It is then left to the discretion of the bishops of this or that people, to enrich these basic forms with elements from previous liturgical practice, or (in the mission countries) from the folk-culture of each land.[3]

This ecumenical Liturgy will be the Liturgy of the day after tomorrow, that is to say, we still have a long and difficult road to travel before reaching that goal. It presupposes not only a world-wide and ecumenical frame of thought, but also a detailed knowledge of the history of Liturgy. A great deal of preparatory work will still be needed. Because of the scarcity of documentary sources, it is more difficult for scholars to get a clear idea of the classical Liturgy of the fourth and fifth centuries, than of the rites of later ages.[4] Besides this, we must be very careful to take the road to an ecumenical Liturgy step by step, without making any sudden break with tradition. And it would certainly be enriching for the Church, if the forms of Liturgy hitherto in use could – on account of their beauty and their antiquity – continue to be cultivated in the future, without change, at least in certain centres, perhaps in cathedrals and in certain monasteries, thus, besides other places, amongst the Benedictines.

Yet the question of Liturgy is in the first instance not a matter of aesthetics, but a matter of pastoral practice: How does worship need to be celebrated, in order to "reach" contemporary people? The producers and broadcasters of the mass media (films, radio, and television) make great efforts to speak to contemporary people. How much more the Church ought to do this in her services of worship, since she has been given the task of preaching the Gospel to all peoples, and of sharing the grace of God with all individuals through the sacraments.

Pius XI once said: "The Church of Christ is neither Latin, nor Greek, nor Russian, but Catholic." It is no longer a matter of whether the Liturgy is celebrated according to

---

3. This idea which I expressed at that time (1964) has widely been put into practice.

4. An example may be offered, for instance, by the African Liturgy of Saint Augustine's time; cf. Klaus Gamber, *Ordo missae africanae. Der nordafrikanische Meßritus zur Zeit des hl. Augustinus* [*The North African Mass Rite in the time of Saint Augustine*], in: *Römische Quartalschrift* no. 64 (1969), pp. 139-153.

a Latin or a Greek rite. The only decisive point will be this, that it must be ecumenical, that it finally bursts the bonds which have fettered it since the time when its form congealed in the Middle Ages. That it looks back to and reflects on its classical period, and at the same time thinks about the requirements of pastoral practice in the wider world. Such a genuine renewal of the Liturgy will not be easy. And yet we must dare to attempt it.